Prayers
From the Heart

By
Reb Moshe Steinerman

Edited by Elise Teitelbaum

כאיל תערג על אפיקי מים כן נפשי תערג אליך אלוקים

"As a hart cries out in thirst for the springs of water, so does my soul cry out in thirst for You, O' HaShem." (Psalms 42:2)

Photo by Reb Moshe Steinerman

Reb Moshe Steinerman

Ilovetorah Jewish Outreach Network

ilovetorah Jewish Publishing
First Published 2018
ISBN: 978-1-947706-07-1

Editor: Elise Teitelbaum
Co Editor: Rochel Steinerman

Artwork by Boris Shapiro
Book Format by Rabbi Benyamin Fleischman

Dedication

In Memory of my father Shlomo Zavel Ben Yaakov zt"l
In Memory of my father-in-law Menachem Ben Ruvain zt"l
And all the great souls of our people

I grew up in a house filled with the Torah learning of my father, who studied most of the day. Although there were no Jews in this remote part of Maryland, my father was a man of *chesed* to all people and was known for his brilliance in Torah scholarship.

Dedicated to my wife Rochel
and to my children Shlomo Nachman, Yaakov Yosef, Gedalya Aharon Tzvi, Esther Rivka, Yeshiya Michel, Dovid Shmuel, and Eliyahu Yisrael.
May it bring forth the light of your neshamos.

Dear Reader,

Ilovetorah Jewish Outreach is a non-profit and books and Torah classes are available at low costs. Therefore, we appreciate your donation to help Rabbi Moshe Steinerman and ilovetorah to continue their work on behalf of the Jewish people. We also ask that you pass on these books to others once you are finished with them.

Thank you,
Reb Moshe Steinerman
www.ilovetorah.com
Donations:
www.ilovetorah.com/donations

Haskamahs / Approbations

בס"ד

RABBI DOVID B. KAPLAN
RABBI OF WEST NEW YORK
5308 PALISADE AVENUE • WEST NEW YORK, NJ 07093
201-867-6859 • WESTNEWYORKSHUL@GMAIL.COM

דוד ברוך הלוי קאפלאן
רב ואב"ד דק"ק
וועסט ניו יארק

י' שבט ה'תשע"ז / February 6, 2017

Dear Friends,

Shalom and Blessings!

For approximately twenty years I have followed the works of Rabbi Moshe Steinerman, Shlit"a, a pioneer in the use of social media to encourage people and bring them closer to G-d.

Over the years Rabbi Steinerman has produced, and made public at no charge, hundreds of videos sharing his Torah wisdom, his holy stories, and his touching songs. Rabbi Steinerman has written a number of books, all promoting true Jewish Torah spirituality. Rabbi Steinerman's works have touched many thousands of Jews, and even spirituality-seeking non-Jews, from all walks of life and at all points of the globe.

Rabbi Steinerman is a tomim (pure-hearted one) in the most flattering sense of the word.

I give my full approbation and recommendation to all of Rabbi Steinerman's works.

I wish Rabbi Steinerman much success in all his endeavors.

May G-d bless Rabbi Moshe Steinerman, his wife, Rebbetzin Rochel Steinerman, and their beautiful children; and may G-d grant them health, success, and nachas!

With blessings,

Rabbi Dovid B. Kaplan

Approval of the Biala Rebbe of New York / Miami / Betar, Israel

הובא לפני גליונות בעניני קירוב רחוקים לקרב אחינו בני ישראל אל
אביהם שבשמים, כידוע מהבעש"ט זיע"א שאמר "אימתי קאתי מר
לכשיפוצו מעינותיך חוצה" ואפריון נמטי"ה להאי גברא יקירא מיקירי
צפת עיה"ק תובב"א כמע"כ מוהר"ר משה שטיינרמן שליט"א אשר כבר
עוסק רבות בשנים לקרב רחוקים לתורה וליהדות, וכעת מוציא לאור
ספר בשם "תפילות הלב" וראיתי דברים נחמדים מאוד וניכר מתוך
הדברים שהרב בעל המחבר - אהבת השי"ת ואהבת התורה וישראל
בלבבו, ובטחוני כי הספר יביא תועלת גדולה לכל עם ישראל.

ויה"ר שיזכה לבוא לגומרה ברוב פאר והדר ונזכה לגאולתן של ישראל
בב"א.

בכבוד רב:
אהרן שלמה חיים אליעזר
בלאאו"ר זצללה"ה אבי'אלא

8

Rabbi M. Lebovits
Grand Rabbi of
Nikolsburg
53 Decatur Avenue
Spring Valley, N.Y. 10977

יוסף יחיאל מיכל
לעבאוויטש
ניקלשבורג
מאנטי - ספרינג וואלי, נ. י.

בעזהשי"ת

בשורותי אלו באתי להעיד על מעשה אומן, מופלא מופלג בהפלגת חכמים ונבונים,
ירא וחרד לדבר ה', ומשתוקק לקרב לבות ישראל לאביהם שבשמים,
ה"ה הרב **משה שטיינערמאן** שליט"א בעיה"ק צפת תובב"א

שעלה בידו להעלות על הספר דברים נפלאים שאסף מספרים הקדושים, בענין אהבה
אחוה שלום וריעות, לראות מעלית חברינו ולא חסרונם, ועי"ז להיות נמנעים מדברי
ריבות ומחלוקת, ולתקן עון שנאת חנם אשר בשביל זה נחרב בית מקדשינו
ותפארתינו, וכמשאחז"ל (רש"י. ויקרא רבה כ"ו ג) על ויחן שם ישראל, שניתנה תורה באופן
שהחנו שם כאיש אחד בלב אחד.

וניכר בספר כי עמל ויגע הרבה להוציא מתח"י דבר נאה ומתוקן, ע"כ אף ידי תכון
עמו להוציאו לאור עולם. ויהי רצון שהפץ ה' בידו יצליח, ויברך ה' חילו ופעול ידו
תרצה, שיברך על המוגמר להגדיל תורה ולהאדירה ולהפיצו בקרב ישראל, עד ביאת
גוא"צ בב"א

א"ד הכותב לכבוד התורה ומרביציה.
ר"ט חשון תשמ"ו

9

Rabbi Abraham Y. S. Friedman
161 Maple Avenue #C Spring Valley NY 10977
Tel: 845-425-5043 Fax: 845-425-8045

רב דביהמ"ד אמרי"ו ספ"ר קאמאדא
וראש כלל חסי"י

בעזהשי"ת

ישפות השם החיים והשלו', לכבוד ידידי מאז ומקדם מיקירי קרתא
דירושלים יראה שלם, זוכה ומזכה אחרים, להיות דבוק באלקינו, ה"ה
הר"ר משה שטיינרמאן שליט"א.

שמחתי מאד לשמוע ממך, מאתר רחוק וקירוב הלבבות, בעסק
תורתך הקדושה ועבודתך בלי לאות, וכה יעזור ה' להלאה ביתר שאת
ויתר עז. והנה שלחת את הספר שלקטת בעניני דביקות בה', לקרב
לבבות בני ישראל לאבינו שבשמים בשפת אנגלית, אבל דא עקא
השפת לא ידענו, ע"כ לא זכיתי לקרותו, ע"כ א"א לי ליתן הסכמה פרטי
על ספרך, ובכלל קיבלתי על עצמי שלא ליתן הסכמות, ובפרט כשאין
לי פנאי לקרות הספר מתחלתו עד סופו, אבל בכלליות זכרתי לך חסד
נעוריך, היאך הי' המתיקות שלך בעבדות השם פה בעירינו, ובנועם
המדות, וחזקה על חבר שאינו מוציא מתחת ידו דבר שאינו מתוקן,
ובפרט שכל מגמתך להרבות כבוד שמים, שבודאי סייעתא דשמיא
ילווך כל ימיך לראות רב נחת מיוצ"ח ומפרי ידיך, שתתקבל הספר
בסבר פנים יפות אצל אחינו בני ישראל שמדברים בשפת האנגלית
שיתקרבו לאבינו שבשמים ולהדבק בו באמת כאות נפשך, ולהרבות
פעלים לתורה ועבודה וקדושה בדביקות עם מדות טובות, בנייחותא
נייחא בעליונים ונייחא בתחתונים עד ביאת גואל צדק בב"א.

כ"ד ידידך השמח בהצלחתך ובעבודתך

About the Author

Rabbi Moshe Steinerman grew up as a religious Jew on the hillsides of Maryland. During his teenage years, Reb Moshe developed his talent for photography, while connecting to nature and speaking to *HaShem*. He later found his path through Breslav *Chassidus*, while maintaining closeness to the *Litvish* style of learning. He studied in the Baltimore yeshiva, Ner Yisrael; then married and moved to Lakewood, New Jersey. After settling down, he began to write Kavanos Halev, with the blessing of Rav Malkiel Kotler *shlit"a*, Rosh Yeshiva of Beis Medrash Gevoha.

After establishing one of the first Jewish outreach websites, ilovetorah.com in 1996, Reb Moshe's teachings became popular among the full spectrum of Jews, from the unaffiliated to ultra-Orthodox. His teachings, including hundreds of stories of tzaddikim, gained popularity due to the ideal of drawing Jews together. Reb Moshe made aliyah to Tzfat in 2003 and then later in 2012 moved to Jerusalem. He has been helping English-speaking Jews return to Judaism through his hundreds of Jewish videos and audio shiurim. His learning experience includes the completion of both Talmud Bavli and Yerushalmi as well as other important works.

Some of his other books are Kavalos Halev (Meditations of the Heart), Tikkun Shechinah, Tovim Meoros (Glimpse of Light), Chassidus, Kabbalah & Meditation, Yom Leyom (Day by Day), Pathways of the Righteous, A Journey into Holiness, and The True Intentions of the Baal Shem Tov. Thousands have read the advice contained in these books, with life-changing results.

Special thanks to Rabbi Benyamin Fleischman for making the books into print-ready format and to Elise Teitelbaum for helping to edit the books.

Table of Contents

Introduction

Rebbe Nachman taught the greatness of turning your *Torah* study into prayers. He advised that everyone should do *hisbodidus*, meditate by speaking to *HaShem* in his own words.

Reb Noson, his main disciple, composed an entire prayer book called *Likutey Tefillos*, which are prayers based on the *rebbe's Torah* lessons. Some of these prayers are very long and detailed. I have chosen that my supplications be simple.

Some of them are very personal and I never thought I would release them to the public. Some I have composed from my own *Torah* teachings and others are direct from my heart to *HaShem*. I started writing these prayers when I was a single man almost twenty years ago. I hope that when you find yourself in need of a prayer, you will find some comfort in these, finding hope and salvation.

It is interesting how most of us look at each other as having an easier life than our own, but in truth, we all share similar struggles and heartaches. Looking through my writings, I see that others are able to relate to most of them. I believe this is because we all share the same soul root of Adam HaRishon and feel connected to each other.

Just as you can benefit from my inner thoughts and prayers, so I could learn much from your experiences. Throughout the history of our nation, thousands of *rabbis*, the Great Assembly, and ordinary Jews have composed Jewish *nigunim* and *piyutim*, songs, prayers and poems. They have left us a way to better connect to our Creator, by expressing ourselves through prayer. I leave you also with a window into my soul and the challenges I faced; I hope you can benefit from them.

I found it very beneficial to write down the prayers I was saying in my *hisbodidus*. It enabled me to recite them repetitively until I felt *HaShem's* salvation. I too recommend you compose your own prayers and follow the footsteps of the great *tzaddikim* who spoke to *HaShem* in personal prayer daily.

Parnasah and Sustenance

HaShem, You sustain and nourish all living things. Thank You for sustaining me, since my conception and from my mother's womb.

I am suffering greatly due to my current financial state. There are so many things I want to complete, but due to a lack of money, I cannot accomplish my dreams. In fact, I cannot even pay my current bills, and as time passes my debt to others increases. I cannot continue living this way. In an effort to lessen my debt and gain control of my finances, I tried innovative ideas to make money. In the end, it only caused me to be more dejected and even to fall into greater debt. Words cannot express the overwhelming sense of hopelessness I feel, as if all the walls around me, my family and my life are crashing before me. *HaShem*, please help me, save me, for You are the true giver of sustenance to all flesh.

(Written February 9, 2006)

Bringing Others Back to HaShem

HaShem, I want to scream it in the streets and to tell the world that I know our *Torah* is *emes*, truth. I want to literally grab my fellow Jews and shake them until they realize they should be following the code of Jewish law and keeping the *Shabbos*. If I did this though, they wouldn't listen. I need therefore to have the understanding how to bring them close to you and show them the truth. Help me, *HaShem*, to bring many people back to the proper *Torah* path.

The only thing is, how can I bring others back to *HaShem* when I am failing so miserably myself? Bring me back to *Yiddishkeit*, so I can properly bring others with me. To you *HaShem*, I call out for help. We are all starving for *Torah*; help us to realize its importance, and to make the changes in our life that will bring us close to You. Thank You for Your abundant patience with us and especially me.

(Written Approx. 1997)

Snatching Each Day

Thank You, *HaShem*, for hearing my prayer. We are told that, "Nothing remains of a person's life other than what he has snatched for himself each day." (R. Noson's Letter #28) May I be worthy to live 120 years in order to elevate the fallen sparks. I must view this day as if it were my last to serve *HaShem* and do *teshuva* (repentance) while in this world.

HaShem Yisborach, forgive me, pardon me for all of the days I wasted, not attaching myself to You as I should. Let this day be one of growth. It should be filled with *mitzvos*, *Torah* and *tefillah*. Help me to rise up like our holy master, Moshe Rabbeinu, who rose to the utmost point. Let me move up all day; don't let me fall from my *madrega* (level).

Please help me to see myself in a clear light, weighing the good and bad in myself, to make sure I'm improving every day. *HaShem*, only with Your help can I see myself as I should and know where to improve. You have already given me so much; let this action, this prayer be for You, *HaShem*, as Your son has now returned to You!

(Written 14 Cheshvan, 1996)

Torah Memory

HaShem Yisborach, I know so little of Your vast *Torah*. The *Torah* is like a tunnel that never ends. It is like a treasure house full of gold, but one can only grab as much as he can hold at the moment. *HaShem*, I don't know which pieces to take, and they are oh so heavy and hard to grasp. My mind is full of so many obstacles that I can only take pieces that break off in my hand.

There are 613 *mitzvos* which are vessels that can hold these gems for me, but I haven't completed building these vessels yet. My 248 limbs can't carry the gems since I have improperly treated them by tainting their purity. Therefore, the gems I manage to grasp are lost and forgotten, due to the impurities in my mind.

HaShem, please help me to do the 613 *mitzvos*. Let me overcome my *yetzer hara* and become pure once again. Allow me to run through the *Torah* like a jaguar runs for his meal, leaving a trail as I go, that I should not forget a word of *Torah*. *HaShem*, even with all the languages in the world, none of them could describe even one ounce of Your kindness to the world. Thank You, once again, for hearing my prayer.

(15 Cheshvan, 1996)

Finding Salvation Through You

HaShem, You continue to show tremendous patience with me. I do not know how to thank You for this. Please know that it means the world to me that You believe in me.

Some people spend an entire lifetime feeling lost and empty. Trying to mend themselves, they find some comfort in physical or secular things. What they are doing is hiding their troubles, like a drunkard with his bottle of whiskey. Is it really a temporary fix or is it crawling deeper into a pit? So where is this emptiness stemming from? How can I be real with myself?

HaShem, I admit I have tried to solve my problems in this frivolous way and even moments ago I attempted to find happiness in the material, but *HaShem*, I want to be real, I want to be truthful. This moment, I cry out to You, asking, pleading that I find my salvation in You and in the *Torah*. Thank you, *HaShem* for hearing me in my time of need.

(Written 9 Shevat, 2005)

Uman Rosh Hashanah

HaShem, now that You have shown me the light of *Breslav Chassidus*, help me to do my part and be with the *Rebbe* for *Rosh Hashanah*, in Uman. If all You would have given to me was to know of the *Rebbe's* existence, that would have been enough. It is such a gift that I am not one opposed to the *Rebbe* and his teachings, but rather I embrace them; I am so thankful for this. Thank you, *HaShem*, for allowing me to find such a holy movement in Judaism and a *Rebbe*. There is no way I can adequately thank You for this, but my heart is warm with love and thanksgiving.

HaShem Yisborach, the *Rebbe* has said, "My main time is *Rosh Hashanah*." (Sichos Haran 215) The *Rebbe* also said, "My *Rosh Hashanah* is greater than everything... No one should be missing! My very essence is *Rosh Hashanah!*" (Tzaddik #403) *HaShem*, I am afraid of missing Uman. Life brings so many barriers, so many obstacles, and there is so much to constantly overcome. Being with the *Rebbe* for *Rosh Hashanah* means so very much to me. Without this, I don't know how I could possibly get through the entire year.

Rebbe Nachman said, that we travel to *tzaddikim* for *Rosh Hashanah* in order to purify our minds. This brings about kindness and compassion for the entire year. (Likutey Moharan 1,211) *HaShem*, as only You truly know, my mind is full of so many distractions, so much *tuma*, so much confusion. I am going to be judged on *Rosh Hashanah* for all of these actions, *HaShem*, forgive me, for all the things I have done this past year. Every act, every word and every thought that I had this past year You will judge. In actuality, *HaShem*, I should begin repenting now and I will. Oh, how my heart will turn to flesh and then I will be able to repent for everything perfectly. My heart will be so broken, it will melt like the *Shabbos* lights, but yet, I will have such *simcha* because I will be attached to the *Rebbe* and all of his *chassidim*. So *HaShem*, You see my desire, my yearning for *Rosh Hashanah* is with very good intentions.

Rebbe Nachman said, "Anyone who has the privilege of being with the *Rebbe* on *Rosh Hashanah* is entitled to be very, very happy." (Tzaddik, 403) *Simcha*, happiness, leads to *d'vekus*, a spiritual uplifting. I want this *simcha* the *Rebbe* is talking about. My limbs are filled with the *simcha* of Uman, just from speaking about it. Reb Noson once stated, "Even if the road to Uman were paved with knives, I would crawl there just so that I could be by the *Rebbe* for *Rosh Hashanah*." (Siach Sarfei Kodesh 1-590) *HaShem*, I'm not Rav Noson. I can walk through some barriers but only so many. Please give me the financial security to go to Uman, and health, and the inner encouragement, and all the support I need from my family and friends. The *Rebbe* said, "I have already made it my business to take care of the expenses of those who come to me for *Rosh Hashanah.*" (Siach Sarfei Kodesh 1-27)

So *Rebbono Shel Olam*, with all that I have said before You, please, I plead with You, let there be no reason for me to miss *Rosh Hashanah* with my *Rebbe*. Master of the world, I thank You for allowing me to even have the feelings I do for Uman. There are no words or even enough *berachos* to say to thank You for bringing me to the *Rebbe*. I will now sing and dance to You the song of Uman to show You the *emunah*, trust, that I have that You will allow me to be there for *Rosh Hashanah* soon.

(Written 1997)

Kodesh Melava Malka

Holy *Shabbos* queen, please return to us with your glorious splendor, again and again, every week. Let me embrace you as a child embraces his mother, greeting you early, waiting to see, feel, and taste your splendor. I love you; you were first in *HaShem's* thoughts and now I also place you first in mine.

In radiant garments, I dress, and with beautiful robes, I stand before you. A smiling face appears to me as I greet you. The smell of beautiful foods, which are like incense to awaken the soul, I prepare for you. The beautiful air of your holiness surrounds me. Let your holiness remain with me not only throughout every minute of *Shabbos* but let it also extend to my weekday. I will try to do things for you as you are a precious bride whom we should treat with all glory and respect. It pains me to see you leave like this after we enjoyed this holy day together; I mean this with all my heart.

To show you my love for you, as *Shabbos* exits, I make this *Melava Malka* meal. I will eat delicious foods for you, dance and sing the holy tunes of our sages. I will now eat and drink something in your honor. Please, shine your holy light into me and *HaShem*, please give me a successful week of *Torah* and *avodas HaShem*.

(Written 1998 approx.)

Melava Malka 2

Thank You, *HaShem* for giving us the *Shabbos*, allowing us to delight in its glory. May this *Shabbos* be a lasting one, in which its light spreads throughout the coming week. Please bring us to the joy Dovid Hamelech felt during this special night, having rejoiced in life and your goodness. May we sing, dance and delight in a *seuda* in the presence of the *Shechinah* and Dovid Hamelech himself.

Let us extend *Shabbos*, trying not to allow this extra soul, this gift of a *neshamah* that we were blessed with on *Shabbos*, return to its source. We should not release it until the very last minute, having used every moment preciously. May our *luz* bone be strengthened, allowing our bodies the extra strength they need to live in this world and to return during *techias hamaisim* (resurrection of the dead). Please allow it to be strong and solid like the second *luchos*, which shall never be broken.

Our week should be one of personal growth, the performance of many *mitzvos* and *tefillos* said with *kavanah*, *Torah* study learned with love and trust in *HaShem*. May all our worries of the previous week be answered and easily solved. Also, may we greet Eliyahu Hanavi in our generation, this week, now, not only for our sakes but also for Yours, *HaShem*.

Let us now continue to start our week on the correct foot, the RIGHT foot of *Netzach*, which is to arise and climb to *HaShem*. You have given me so much through the sanctity of the *Shabbos*; please allow it to remain with me, even just a small piece of this *kedusha*. Thank You!

(Written after Chanukah 1996)

Pure Dreams

HaShem, I am no *tzaddik* but even so, I must ask that You please give me pure and holy dreams, dreams from paradise, dreams of learning *Torah*, performing the *mitzvos* and truly good things. Let me return for the night, my soul, to be replenished with complete faith in You. When I arise, I should be ready to serve You truthfully. Please forgive my sins and let me easily fall asleep so I may serve you, feeling rejuvenated in the morning when I arise. May my sleep be considered real *avodas HaShem*, as I only go to bed now in order to serve You better. Thank You for giving me the opportunity to serve You this past day. I am now making a new beginning as I sit here about to retire to sleep. *HaShem* I love you!

Going to Israel and Repentance

HaShem, I am on my way to *Eretz Yisrael*. So many *tzaddikim* and *Torah* giants never received the gift of performing the *mitzvah* to walk four cubits in the holy land. How can someone as low as I am, and from the dust of the earth, be allowed to go and fulfill this *mitzvah*?

HaShem, I am not complaining, but rather I am wondering, how can I ever repay You for your kindness to me? I am having so many thoughts of repentance; please forgive me for my all my sins, especially the first sins I committed which led to repetitious sins of the same nature. The first time I showed anger, spoke improperly, dishonored my parents, let down my guard with *tikkun habris* and purity, had thoughts of pride, performed a negative commandment, neglected a positive commandment, skipped a *beracha*, didn't put on *tallis* and *tefillin*, said Your name in vain, hurt my fellow Jew, lied, ate for the wrong reasons, didn't honor the festivals or mourning periods, failed to give *ma'aser* (10% to charity), got depressed or didn't pray when I was supposed to. Again, please forgive my first sins and all those that have followed. Please arouse your thirteen attributes of mercy to forgive, pardon, and release me from my *avairos*, and let me make a fresh start (today).

Draw me near to You, and to the true *tzaddikim* in Israel and abroad. I'm trying to leap towards You; catch me in the net of the *Torah*. Let me find a new recognition of Your glory and the truth of the *Torah*. Please let my learning remain with me. I'm nothing, nothing at all. Have joy impress itself upon my heart. Rebuild the holy Temple. I await the Mashiach's coming NOW.

(Written approx., Teves 1997)

Bring Me Close

Abishter oh *Abishter*, bring me close to You! Shine Your countenance on me. Let me not be like one who wastes his days away. Help me recognize my mission in life.

May the paths I take be paths of truth. Please grant me holy visions. Oh how wonderful it is to open a *sefer* and receive guidance directly from *Shamayim* (the Heavens). *HaShem* it is so easy to get lost; let me not be like one who strays. Let there be no more grief in the world. The *Torah* is too precious; let me be the one to spread it.

How can we thank You for all You have done for us? Let me serve You and love You, as Your holy patriarchs did. My fear of Heaven should be pure and everlasting. Help me to sing, compose songs to Your name with great *da'as* (understanding), and express true love and fear of Heaven. Let my voice and *shirim* (songs) help arouse others to *avodas HaShem* and *teshuvah*. Help me to purify each of the four elements I am composed of. Allow my heart to return to Your ways, *Amen*!

(Written 6/25/97)

No More Confusion

HaShem, I'm in a state of confusion. Please give me the wisdom to get out of this detrimental mind state. I love You and I want to serve You, but I just don't know how because of my current circumstances.

Please *HaShem*, let everything start to make sense to me, and bring me back to You. "If I will return to You, You will return to me." (Zechariah 1:3) Where can I find *HaShem's* glory? My *simcha* (joy) is lacking. Please give me *shefa* (sustenance) to bring up my spirit. *HaShem* is with me! I shall not fear, for my deliverance and sustenance is on its way.

HaShem, You who feed all flesh will certainly not overlook me in my time of need. Thank You for allowing me to speak from my heart about my troubles.

(Written 6/1/97)

Patience, *Emunah*, and Faith

HaShem, if only I took the time to think, I would improve myself and become a good Jew.

Forgive me for this impatience that I have. It stems from my lack of trust that You always do what is best. If I truly feared You as I should I wouldn't be so impatient, because I would be occupied in *mitzvos* and learning *Toras HaShem.*

Forgive me, forgive me; I am sorry *HaShem.* But this world, with all its trials and tribulations, is so hard to bear. Please continue to do what is best for me. I will improve my *emunah* and be more patient. As I know, salvation is on the way! Think good and it will be good. Your servant, a drop in the ocean, _____ (your name).

(Written May 1997)

I Am a Jew and Not A Heathen

Look up, and you will see He is there. *HaShem* hasn't hidden Himself. You're standing before the King of Kings, *HaShem* who is One. You have nothing to fear; *HaShem* is near! Don't swallow yourself up; it solves nothing. Be good and be happy. You're a Jew and not a heathen. What else is there to say? You're a Jew and not a heathen!

Don't be ashamed; you are part of the greatest nation in the world. You are a *Yid!* You were given the jewel of all jewels on Mt. Sinai. The *Torah's* commandments are all bright lights. You think your path is dark, but if you really look around the light is so bright it could blind your eyes. No, don't place dimmers over your eyes; it is okay to look! Look and you will see it is all there in front of you to see!

(Written May 1997)

I Must Not Surrender

Rebbono Shel-Olam, You are so good to me with all that You do. *HaShem*, let my evil inclination surrender itself to You. I don't want to do bad anymore; I only want to do good.

I hate sinning and I despise evil. I want no part of the evil temptations in the world. Life is too short, and our days are all too precious. Certainly, I do not want to waste it away with evil. Even a hairsbreadth in which we improve ourselves is miles of achievement in *Shamayim*.

HaShem will lead us in the path we want to go. Master of the world, I want to go on the pathway of purity, *Torah*, *mitzvos* and *avodas HaShem*. I love *HaShem* and I hate evil, and sin!! Let my heart be aroused to serve You always! Thank You for hearing my prayers and the pains from my heart.

(Written April 20, 1997)

Baruch Hashem, Baruch Hashem

Baruch HaShem; Baruch HaShem; Baruch HaShem; Baruch HaShem; HaShem, I love You.

If I could hug You, I would never let You go. You're compassionate and so kind to me. You sustain me; you give me life, breath, the *Torah, chassidus* and comfort. You give me the *mitzvos* that are so special, like *tzitzis, tefillin* and *mezuzos*. You've created beautiful surroundings for me to look at; nature and its wondrous details. Constantly, Your hand is sustaining me in every way.

You love me, and You love your people. Always You are protecting us, sustaining us, sheltering us, giving us food and drink, clothing, a roof, a car and music to uplift us. Not just regular music, but also Divine melodies, which are the greatest in the world.

Oh, let me come close to You, *HaShem*. Please let nothing stand in my way and hold me back from being near to You. Compared to You, I am nothing. Without You, I don't exist. Thank You, Thank You... *Halleluka*!

(Written April 1997)

34

I Am Nothing

Oy *HaShem*, I am nothing. I am no better than anyone else. I am nothing more than dust and ashes. Even this tree outside my house is taller than I am. I barely take up any space in this material world; how much less in *Shamayim*.

When I look around, there are people wiser and smarter than I am. What have I learned; maybe ten or so *sefarim* out of thousands? Obviously, I am totally nothing. Searching myself though, I do have many good points, but this can't make me think I am a *tzaddik*. I'm important to *HaShem*, but I am far from being a *benoni* (intermediate man).

The entire world could be completely balanced on the scale of judgment, and I could make the entire difference for everyone. My one *mitzvah* could bring the *Mashiach* this very moment. I just have to fill this day with one *mitzvah* after another. Please *HaShem*, bless your holy people with sustenance, their *bashert*, children, and great *tzaddikim* to lead us. *HaShem*, I love You and I thank You for all you have done for me, a simple drop in the ocean.

(Approx. April 1997)

Finding A Rope

If I return to *HaShem*, *HaShem* will return to me. (*Malachi 3:7*) Should I become lost in the unholy depths, *HaShem* is there to lift me up. There is no place where *HaShem* cannot be found: Everywhere I go, *HaShem* is there.

If only I didn't feel I had to search so much to find You; but really, You are nearer to me than I realize. Sometimes when I feel You are furthest away, You are really the closest.

HaShem, please console me in Your kindness and grant me the strength to carry on. *HaShem*, if only You would send me a rope, I would climb out of this pit I am stuck in. You allowed me to fall, so I ask, "Where can I find *HaShem's* glory?" Then You embrace me, picking me back up and out of the depth, I fell into. If I do not fall occasionally, I cannot go up. Falling only helps me to grow.

Please, *HaShem*, help me find a rope; don't allow me to drown in my faults and self-pity. Accept my inner feelings and repentance when I recite the simple words of, "Where can I find Your glory?" *HaShem*, my Creator, King, and Healer. When I grab Your life line, please harness me with Your glory. Let me fulfill the goodness of creation and climb higher in my service of You. May I be blessed to elevate *Malchus* to its source. Now that I am elevated, allow me to serve You with all the proper intentions taught by *chazal*. Thank You, *HaShem* for hearing my troubles and for lifting the fallen.

(Adar 13, 1995)

Learning Torah Lishmah/ Finished Sefer

HaShem, Your kindness has helped me complete a wonderful measure of learning. Thank You, *Hashem*; may I continue on this path and grow in *avodas HaShem*.

Please let me remember everything I learned. Let me be purified by learning the *Torah*. May the *simcha* (joy) of this completion stay with me and bring me closer to You. My learning is for the sake of unifying the holy One, blessed be He, and His *Shechinah*. May I be able to complete everything I've learned through my actions! All the learning I do in this world will be revealed in the world to come, with great understanding.

Rav Yehoshua ben Karcha never walked four cubits without studying *Torah*, or without wearing *tefillin*. May we strive to attain this level! With *HaShem's* help, we will come closer and closer to it.

Please *HaShem*, grant me sustenance, health, *simcha* (joy) and the free time to learn *Torah* all the days of my life. May I learn with great love for the *Torah* and our Creator; learn *lishmah* (for its own sake), sharing the *Torah* with others, and may it also bring wholeness in my life.

May others around me always be supportive of my learning! It is difficult to learn without peace, and the biggest cause for strife is financial trouble. Please, *Hashem*, let this never be my worry. May I put all the energy you give me into *Torah* study, prayer and *gemilos chasadim*. All of my 248 limbs and sinews should be engulfed in serving *HaShem*.

Thank You, *HaShem* for Your kindness and support. May all that I said find favor in Your eyes and be fulfilled. Amen.

(Written approx. April 1997)

Mitzvah of Soferus

HaShem, could it really be that we are so lenient in the *mitzvos* of *tefillin*, *mezuzos*, and *tzitzis?* How could we have overlooked such simple *mitzvos?* Please help *klal Yisrael* fulfill these *mitzvos* with stringency. This includes checking, writing, buying, hanging, wearing, and kissing our *tefillin*, *mezuzos*, and *tzitzis.* May we do all aspects of these *mitzvos* properly, as taught to us by Moshe Rabbeinu, on *Har Sinai.*

May we have a new awareness of their importance and reach higher levels of *yiras Shamayim.* Please remove our suffering and give us a new *mazal* of blessing in our life. Thank You, *HaShem* for hearing my prayers.

(Written 8 Adar *bais*, 1997)

Prayer of Mincha

HaShem, I am about to place on the Altar the *tefillah*, *mincha* prayer service of Yitzchok. I could recite it in a normal fashion as I always have, but instead, I will make it something new.

This will be a unique prayer, never before has it been uttered with these emotions and thoughts. My soul will give over to the *malachim* something they have never interpreted before. May all of the aspects of my prayer, those from now and those from the past, go through the gates of *Shamayim*. I will not rush this prayer and will pronounce each word properly.

"*HaShem*, please open my lips and my mouth will declare Your praise." (Psalms 51:18)

(Adar 1997)

Before Prayer

Please *HaShem*, have my *tefilla* break through all the barriers I've created, which separate me from my Creator. Allow my prayer to bring me closer to You and therefore, let me receive all that You wanted to give me. You already intended to give me all that I prayed for. It was only because of me, that I put distance between us, through evil deeds, that You did not answer my requests.

Please help me express the hidden secret of מנצפ״ך (see my Kabbalah *sefer* for explanation): The Gutturals, Palatals, Linguals, Dentals, and Labials, with all my strength. This is a new *tefilla* that has never been recited before with the same emotions. Please open the gates and the chambers with every breath I exhale. Let my faith increase with every letter I utter. Let me stand in the place where the *Shechinah* waits to be rectified. Also, let Her stay with me throughout the day.

May the *kavanah* of this prayer increase from those I recited previously. May I grow spiritually and as a person through each and every word I recite. Thank You, *HaShem* who hears the prayers of His people.

(Written in 1997)

40

Reb Moshe Steinerman

Prayers for Chatzos

2000 Years is Enough, The *Kotel* Cries Out!

It has been 2000 years since I was erect and standing in my glory. I no longer see the *Kohanim* standing in their beautiful long robes. The *Levyim*, oh how I miss their beautiful songs. The simple Israelites, oh how I miss the way they served our Creator.

How much longer will it be? The Arabs have built their homes next to the holy walls, against my will and want. Jews, how can you stand idly by while all this takes place? My *Yidden*, how much longer will you stand by in sin the days pass that we could be enjoying the splendor of the *Bais Hamikdash* and its service? When will you repent and release me from my imprisonment?

HaShem, your people have been sighing over me for so many years. We want you *HaShem* and You only. Let the *Torah* and all the 613 *mitzvos*, those which we can complete in this exile and those reserved for the times of *Mashiach*, let them be completed. All the necessary rectifications should happen immediately, and we should see the *Mashiach*!

(Written Cheshvan 1997)

Oy Salvation

HaShem, You are always there for me, listening and accepting my prayers. Oy, *HaShem*, my heart... aw, my body and soul cries out feeling sick. Help all of us; don't continue to turn us away. We are suffering too much from this bitter exile. If only You would bring us the salvation we long for. There are just too many people I know who are ill.

Please *HaShem*, it is enough suffering. Turn our mourning into gladness. Bring our limbs to burst out in dancing before you. Elevate our soul to a new level. Give us a complete salvation. We're Jews, *baruch HaShem*. *HaShem* is One - the King, Helper, Deliverer, and our Shield. We shall lack nothing and tomorrow we will all be in Jerusalem, at the *Bais Hamikdash*. There we will dance, singing a new tune that will touch our hearts like never before. *HaShem*, we will be One and Your name One. oy *Mashiach HaShem*!

(8 Adar *bais*, 1997)

Arise, Cry Out

Arise, cry out at night during the beginning of the watches! Pour out your heart like water in the presence of *HaShem*. Join the angels and the *tzaddikim* in praising *Hakadosh baruch Hu* during the most precious and beautiful watches. Just as the *malachim* of the previous watch have stepped down from their posts, so must we push our previous thoughts and activities behind us. What a privilege it is to be awake at this precious hour. Please help me utilize it to my fullest potential and not waste a precious moment of this time. Assist me in truly learning *Torah lishmah* and praying to You with the utmost devotion. Others may sleep away their days (Psalms 59), ואני אשיר עזך but as for me, I will sing of your strength וארנן לבקר חסדך and I will sing aloud in the morning of your kindness.

(Written 1997)

At Night His Song is With Me

The kindness *HaShem* has given by allowing us to open our mouths in prayer is beyond our comprehension. The only way to know how much *yiras Shamayim* you have is to go into the mountain forest at *chatzos* and do *hisbodidus*. Your mouth will open, and words will flow forth to *HaShem*, similar to rains rushing down the mountainside. It is enough to go out to the forest for even a few minutes and yearn to be close to the Creator, for each time you go, you will understand *Chassidus* greater and greater. The *Rebbe's* (The Baal Shem Tov and Rebbe Nachman's) spirit will be real to you; their teachings will come alive as never before.

Chatzos is a time of great favor from *HaShem* and I shouldn't allow it to slip by. Help me, *HaShem*, to go to bed during the first watch of the night so I can arise during the third one to praise You with the *malachim* (angels). I want to recite the *Tikkun*, do *hisbodidus*, learn *Torah* and evaluate myself every night. May I not let this valuable time slip by without performing truthful *avodas HaShem*. My *davening* in the morning should not be affected by this devotion, or the peace within my home.

יומם יצוה ה חסדו ובלילה שירה עימי תפילה לקל חי

During the day, *HaShem*'s kindness is with me and during the night His song. May I look to *Shamayim* in the mornings and draw down *da'as* (understanding). Thank You, *HaShem* for giving us this special time when we can serve You and draw near to You.

(Written, November 4, 1996)

How Much Longer?

HaShem, how much longer do we have to wait for the *Bais HaMikdash* to be rebuilt? It has been so long that we are in exile, over 2000 years. We are lonely, *mamash* we are lonely and miss the holiness of the *Bais HaMikdash*. One stone of the *Bais HaMikdash* is more precious than all the jewels of the world.

Oh, to hear the *Levyim* singing and playing new songs to *HaShem*. Oh, to see the *Kohanim* dressed in the *bigdei kahuna* and the *Yisraelim* who are so dear to *HaShem*. To return home in peace and tranquility is my greatest dream. There could be just one curtain remaining in the *Kodesh HaKedoshim* waiting to be rectified [and then everything would be complete for the redemption]. (Baal Divrei Chaim)

HaShem, help us to do the remaining rectifications quickly and please, if we are just shy a little from its completion, *HaShem*, You complete the rest for us. You have always helped us in the past, *HaShem*, we need You!

(Nissan 1995)

Rebuild Our House

Master of the World, a house without the cries of children is more destroyed than the holy Temple. A house without joy and singing is empty. Too many people are suffering with the barrenness and remain alone.

How much longer must we continue to be tested until we prove ourselves worthy of redemption? How long must we wait and cry bitter tears? Is our yearning not enough? How can we make ourselves a complete vessel for Your holiness? *HaShem*, please lead us in the path of up-rightness, purity and holiness. *HaShem*, when will we all gather together? *Tzion* is barren and desolate of the holiness it once had. We as a nation have suffered so greatly. We have been misjudged and emotionally scarred by the multitudes.

How can we elevate the remaining sparks? Unify that which is left and stuck in the unholy realms? When will we ourselves be unified? Bear fruit and break the shell? A town without the cries of children will be destroyed. Will the gates and doors we have now open into *Yerushalayim*? Has it rained on the garden enough? If not for us, hasn't *HaShem* been lonely enough without His home glorified? Are all the righteous in *Olam Habah* (the World to Come), and this world, not enough?

It is time! *Mashiach* is close! Let us yearn more than ever. Together with the righteous in *Gan-Eden* we can do it. We will soon be singing a new song! Each of our 248 limbs will dance before You, *HaShem*. We will soon be answered. Let us join together to bring the holy *Mashiach*, all of us as one, a nation of holiness. It will be just like the *Rebbono shel-Olam* has promised.

(7 Adar 1995)

46

Prayers to Find One's Bashert

Shidduchim, marriage, it is very difficult and an all new ball game for me, *HaShem*. I do not want to fail in my *avodas HaShem* because of my attention to a *shidduch*. That is not the purpose; it is supposed to be a very holy thing. Let me fulfill this *mitzvah* with purity from now on; don't let the search for a *shidduch* have a negative effect on my holiness.

What do I have to do to understand that there is no reason to sin; it is all in my head, the other side's trick to get me to stumble? No more; it is enough; *HaShem* rebuke *Satan*! Let my mind be filled with *Torah* at all times. *Torah* heals and purifies. Help me so that my *Torah* learning should be done with joy, grace and purity. What else is there besides *Torah* and *mitzvos*? What else is important?!

HaShem, protect me; be with me always. Please don't test me through *shidduchim* and other things. Also, don't let me test myself. So many things are simply the trick of the *yetzer hara*. Let me not fear anything, since You are near to me. Please, bring me my *bashert* soon. Thank you *HaShem*, for without your help, I could not overcome this test of *Shidduchim*.

(Written 6/26/97)

Prayer for Future Bashert (For Men)

HaShem, You already chose my *bashert*. I don't know where she is holding in her *Yiddishkeit*, but I'm sure she is beginning to show signs of a beautiful *bas Yisrael*. Wherever she is, please allow her to be successful. Please remove all sorrow and difficulties from her path and lead her toward becoming a *tzaddekis* (righteous woman). May she never question what the *Torah* says is right. The paths she takes should always be of truth. Her words should be spoken with wisdom, understanding, kindness and grace. Never would she think about speaking idly. Her modesty, patience, *chesed* and inner beauty should shine forth and be an example to all. She should follow the footsteps of Sara with her arms open wide. Like Rivka, she should break the atheism in this world and bring people back to serving their creator. Even for animals she was willing to muster up all her strength to care for them. Her *hachnasas orchim* (hospitality to others) spoke for itself. May her reachable goals be comparable to her great mother Rivka. The accomplishments our mothers reached could not have been without the support and encouragement of their husbands. May I be such a strong pillar to support such a vessel of holiness! Also, may our home be one of compromise, not of *Torah* values, but in search for truth. May we be blessed with numerous kids brought into this world with holiness. May they honor the *Torah* and their parents like Yosef ha Tzaddik! *Hashem*, there's only one problem with these hopes and dreams: I AM STILL ALONE!

(Written 8 Adar *bais*, 1997)

I Search for My Bashert

HaShem, I search far and wide with no relief. Where is she, the one I am supposed to hold so dear? I've gone through communities, *shuls*, *shadchanim*, friends, and even crossed oceans looking for her.

HaShem, You separated us and led us in different directions from the time of our birth. You made a map with the exact course for us to find one another, but You are the only One that can read it. I stop to ask directions from *rabbanim*, friends, *shadchanim*, but they only seem to lead me in the wrong direction. It is so painful to put my heart on the line, only to end up at a dead end. But I/we have hope and we try again because the *Rebbe* says, each encounter, even each suggestion, brings our intended partner closer.

Please let my suffering cease and give me a sprout of deliverance. *HaShem*, You have always helped me and been there for me in my time of need. *HaShem*, I am needy.

(Written 8 Adar *bais*, 1997)

Man Should Not Be Alone

HaShem, the *Torah* says: "It is not good for man to be alone." (Genesis 2:18) Loneliness leads to sin and depression. I do not want to have a problem with these things. I'm selfish, I have anger, no patience, and I don't know how to compromise. These things I developed from being alone so long.

HaShem is One, and *HaShem* created the Jewish people to enjoy the *mitzvos*, and His desire is to share some of His glory. So too, I, _____ (your name) need to share and enjoy the company of another. The world exists only because of the breath of the children. (Talmud Shabbos 119b) It says, *HaShem* listens to the cries of children. When *HaShem* hears their study, He enjoys it more than the learning of adults. So too, I enjoy the laughter, studying and joy of children; this is one of the greatest *mitzvos* in the *Torah*.

Please grant me my wife so I may also fulfill this awesome *mitzvah*. This will bring both of us happiness, *HaShem*. May it be your will that I find her right away!

(7 Adar *bais*, 1997)

Soul Mate

HaShem, how can I continue to serve You in such a state of despair? I'm lonely, I'm broken, I'm incomplete, I'm unhappy, my soul is sick, and my body is in shambles. How much longer will I have to wait for my *bashert*, my partner in life and the completion of my soul? How can I begin to understand the unity with my creator when I am still unassembled in the lowly world? How can I be completely devoted to *HaShem* when my soul is separated from its complete essence?

I can't perfect all my attributes if I have no one to help me. I need the help of my soul-mate to get me through this bitter exile. The trials and tribulations are too much to bear alone. I know it's not You *HaShem* holding back Your kindness, but my deeds that are holding back my salvation. So *HaShem*, I am making a clean start. I will stop this unlawful behavior and devote myself to *avodas HaShem*. I will guard the *bris* (covenant with *HaShem*) and increase my levels of purity daily.

May I recite my prayers in the right way, with faith, truth and simplicity, binding myself to the *tzaddik*! Also, may I always find openings through the flood waters and recite my prayers with absolute devotion. Please let the arrival of my *zivug* be imminent. I shall fear no one but my Creator, and Him I shall fear with every breath I take. "I believe with perfect faith that *HaShem* is One; First, Last and Always!" (Sefer Hamidos)

(7 Adar *bais*, 1997)

I Want A Family

Rebbono Shel-Olam (Master of the world), You have created us in Your image so that we may dwell in Your greatness and glory. *HaShem*, You brought us into this world to share in Your glory in the World to Come, and ultimately *l'yemos HaMashiach*. You chose us as Your nation and gave us the precious *Torah* and its commandments. What a pleasure it is to be a drop in the ocean, a part of the people You call *B'nei Yisrael* (the children of Israel).

The first commandment in the *Torah* is to be *HaShem*'s *shaliach* (messenger) and bring a precious child into this world. What an honor it is that You entrusted us with this great *mitzvah*! Rebbe Nachman says, "A person is not successful until he has children." The pleasure of raising *yiras Shamayim* (G-d fearing) children, to teach them the *Torah* and allow them to one day fulfill this *mitzvah* themselves, is beyond words. It is so difficult to learn *Torah* and not to be able to express it to children.

Oh, the joy that's missing from my life because I stand here alone, unable to have children. How much longer will it be until I can have the family I long for? *HaShem*, what joy we could bring each other. Please let me be the one to raise your *tzaddikim* and *tzaddkaniyos*.

Reunite my *neshamah* with its missing pieces. Lead me in the direction of finding my *bashert*. Let her possess the qualities of our great mothers, Sara, Rivka, Rochel and Leah. Every day we await one another is a day lost, when we could be teaching our children and grandchildren *Torah*. Help us to be ready to receive the gift of success. May we guard the covenant with all our strength and soon bring the final reunion of *Keter* and *Malchus*. May we see the *Mashiach* in our days. Thank You, *HaShem* for hearing my prayer and for understanding my troubles.

(Written, 2 Sivan, 1997)

Shabbos Preparation

The holy *Shabbos* is so special; what a gift you have given us with its weekly blessing. You know, if we had the Torah but we were not given the *zechus* of *Shabbos*, life, *avodas HaShem* would still be remarkable. But *Shabbos* is not only an added blessing; we are told it is the center of our world, the center of our Judaism.

So how can I enter the *Shabbos* with so much physicality, so much grief tied to my bones? All week long I am surrounded with the craziness of the current world, yet I am too weary to just release it all and let go of my troubles.

I ask You *HaShem*, to help me be a vessel to receive this holy light of *Shabbos*. Certainly, I understand its greatness, and that is the problem; it is something beyond my ability to conceive or cherish. Its light is more than I can take in, and I am scared I will not appreciate it or observe the day properly.

When You gave the Jewish people this gift, *HaShem*, You understood that we would struggle to attire ourselves with the necessary purity to observe this holy day. But You also availed this holiness to each of us on whatever plane we were holding in our life.

The thing is, *Shabbos* is compared to the world to come. It shares some of the same light. You know something special? *Chazal* say that the world to come can be attained in an instant. That's right, one moment of repentance and you can enter into the greatest light. So too it is with *Shabbos*; it just takes one moment of the proper preparation to enter into *Shabbos*... how great it is though when we prepare ourselves all day or even all week. But can you imagine the person whose whole life is a preparation for *Shabbos*?

Well if *Shabbos* is truly a gift, why should we even need to prepare for it?

Once there was a king who invited all his people into the castle, to receive a special gift. He did this in order to bond with the people. Obviously, the people wouldn't just show up to see the king in normal attire or without cutting their hair.

The people who truly understood the importance of the King would spend the entire week preparing for the meeting. We do the same with *Shabbos*; even though it is given to us as a gift, we prepare ourselves to receive it.

May I be such a holy servant! Thank You, HaShem for this wonderful gift!

Tefilla for Avodas HaShem
Prayers from Sefer Kavanos Halev

HaShem, thank You so much for giving me the opportunity to serve You with love and to fear Your name. I am taught that fear of Heaven is the beginning of wisdom but, *HaShem*, I am so far from real fear. The great *tzaddikim* would tremble as they said Your holy Name in prayer, while I run through it as if it were just another word. Not only do I lack sufficient awe of Your Name, but I also fail to serve You out of love. At times, I do so by rote and fear alone. My expectations for myself are higher than this; nonetheless, I continue to repeat the error of my ways. I turn to You, *HaShem*, for help, asking, begging to experience the true meaning of *Yiras HaShem* and love for You.

I want to engrave the *pasuk* from Dovid HaMelech, "*Shivisi HaShem linegdi samid,*" in my mind and heart. *HaShem*, You know how difficult it is for me to practice this as my mind constantly wanders from place to place. Only You, *HaShem*, can help me to make this great teaching a reality. Help me, *HaShem*, not to sleep away the days of my life. Assist me in making my heart and service of You authentic. I need Your help and the inner strength to follow all the laws of the Shulchan Aruch. I know how important it is to follow all the laws, but sometimes I become overwhelmed just trying to keep my life in order. My *yetzer hara* can be so strong and convincing that at times I do foolish things. I even shock myself to think, *HaShem*, that while I am making my grievous mistakes, Your sustenance remains my lifeline. I don't understand why You keep providing me with more opportunities when I have failed miserably at the ones You've already given me. Your mercy, love and patience with me are beyond the comprehension of the angels, let alone someone of earthly form.

If only I feared and loved You as I know I should, I would be a much greater person than I am today. When will I merit that the light of the *Shechinah* abides with me? At what point in my life will I finally realize that there is nothing more important than to serve You with love and fear? *HaShem*, please help me to never forget from where I came and before Whom I stand, bowed in gratitude. Help me to avoid a heart full of pride, thinking I'm above my neighbor in honorable deeds. Let me not go through life making excuses for events that surround me; let me realize Your hand in everything and not attribute it to luck or the regular course of nature. Help me to recognize Your Hand in my life, protecting me from evil and mishap. Let me not leave this world without repenting for my sins. Please help me to follow the advice of the great sages, to make an accounting of my actions every evening.

HaShem, it is so important to acquire fear of Heaven. A person can't become a *tzaddik* and grow in his *Yiddishkeit* without proper fear of You. I could serve You without love, but Your glory would never reach into the deepest recesses of my heart. *Rebbono Shel Olam*, You have given us so many reasons to be thankful. Of the thousands of things, You do for us each day, we cannot recognize even a fraction. Please know that we are sincerely grateful.

Tefilla for Simcha

Master of the world, I am grateful for everything You blessed me with. You sustain every creature, from a human being to a tiny fly. Never do You forget my family or me as You continually provide for all of our needs. With everything You give me, I might sometimes forget to be thankful. Some of this stem from the sadness and depression I often slip into. I know there is no reason to be sad, since You provide so well for me, but being human I am far from perfect. I can't say I don't know how to be happy because truly I do. All I have to do is look at my family and friends, but I think about what I lack rather than have, even though I have more than I need.

Help me please *HaShem* in my *emunah* and *bitachon*. I know that my lack of *emunah* is the reason for much of my sadness. We are taught that the greatest joy comes from performing *mitzvos*, especially from the blessing for not being a heathen. As easy as it should be, I live without realizing how fortunate I am. When I perform *mitzvos*, I forget their meaning and importance. Please help me remember and recognize all the good that surrounds me.

Lead me to a life with the utmost joy and harmony in my heart. One way to attain joy is to dance and sing *zemiros*. Sometimes laziness overcomes me, and I don't want to exert myself. Other times I feel embarrassed that my family or friends might see me dancing and make fun of me. This is not a valid excuse, since it would bring joy not only to me but also to others. Please help me to dance and sing with joy and may all my sadness turn to joy. Let the judgments against *Klal Yisrael* and me be full of mercy and not strict *din,* judgment. So many sins weigh heavily on my shoulders; please lighten the weight and help me make a new beginning in my *avodas HaShem*.

Tefillah for Hatzlacha

Master of the world, there is nothing in the world that can compare to You. You are far above all creatures, both in Heaven and on Earth. To talk about You is to belittle all of the things You truly do and can do. You made man out of the simple dust from the earth. A woman You took out of his ribs. From a drop of seed and an egg is created a wondrous embryo. Who is like You *HaShem*, Maker of Heaven and Earth?

I'm just a simple person, *HaShem*, yet I am tested as if I'm a great man. What do I know of the Torah and of being a *tzaddik*? Yet every day my evil inclination works valiantly to make me stumble in my ways. Well I have to admit *HaShem*, I am striving, and I want to be a true servant. But these walls, *HaShem*, how am I to climb them? Do I not hurt when I stumble? Okay, so the only way to come close to You is to be tested and tried, but I am not a criminal. I am mere flesh and blood. I have flesh that bruises easily, and blood that runs hot inside me. Do I mean to defile myself like those who have no covenant with you *HaShem*? I want to be true to myself and my Creator!

HaShem, I do not want to live a double life, one of *Torah* and the other of *tuma*. Our days here on Earth are short. Before we know it, we will be standing before You, giving an account of our every move in this world. What am I going to say *HaShem* when I stand before You in shame? Who will save me and explain that my intentions were good? I just messed up a little bit out of laziness and laxity.

My evil inclination is smart. It knows how to push the right buttons and cause me to really mess up. The *Torah* is the antidote, but I haven't used it. I don't know why, *HaShem*; I have no excuse, no reason to justify all that I have done since I was first created.

HaShem, I have sinned by giving in to my inclination. Save me *HaShem*, help me escape my self-affliction. I don't want to end my days burning from the fire of *Gehinnom*. Instead I would rather control myself in this world and not go after my physical desires. *HaShem*, rebuke *Satan*. Destroy him and return him to his place. Demolish him from the face of the Earth!

Help me *HaShem* to falter no more, especially over impure desires. They are a striving after wind and give no true satisfaction. The only contentment is in *Torah* and righteous deeds. Everything else is fruitless and vanity.

Prayers of the Heart

Please help me to say the *Tikkun HaKlali* and may it purify every limb of my body. When I use the *mikvah* with the true intentions of cleanliness in mind and body. Let my *Torah* learning be a true protection and antidote from all troubles. When I'm confused, help me run to you *HaShem*. Assist me in finding teachers I can confide in who will inspire me to repent-- not only to tell me to repent, but also to show me how.

HaShem, as You can see, I want only You. My heart might be confused but it is true to You. Take me back *HaShem* and rest Your *Shechinah* upon me. Forgive me, merciful *HaShem*. Thank You for all Your patience.

Prayer for Torah Study

Thank You, *HaShem* for giving me the strength and time to learn. I am grateful that You created me as a Jew and have given me one *mitzvah* equivalent to all 613 commandments. A *mitzvah* is so precious to me that I am pleading to You, *HaShem*, to allow me to fulfill it in all of its particulars, learning *Torah* for its own sake and without ulterior motives, to study with joy and serenity. Please give me *shalom* with those around me so I can concentrate and not be distracted. Please *HaShem*, take away the worries of *parnasa* and give my family sufficient income so I can devote myself to *Torah* study.

Rebbono shel Olam, help me please to teach and practice the *Torah* I learn so it won't be lost. Help me understand and remember everything I learn so as to fulfill it in all its aspects.

The *yetzer hara* is constantly on the chase to prevent me from learning. Instead of failing to strengthen myself as I should, let the *Satan* fall from his attempts at preventing me from study. *HaShem*, I truly want to study Your *Torah* and I do not want to waste away my days in pointless, frivolous things. I know that I can do better *HaShem* but not without Your constant assistance. *HaShem*, I am calling for help from the deepest depths of my heart. Honestly *HaShem*, it's not that I don't know how to serve You and overcome my evil inclination. I do know! I'm being realistic by asking for Your assistance, as I am sick of failing You *HaShem*, and failing my forefathers, parents and myself. I can try fooling myself all I want, but when it really comes down to it most of my problems stem from *bitul Torah*. Master of the world, help me to use my time properly from now on, not wasting one minute on unimportant things. *Torah* is first, *Torah* is last, and it is true happiness!

I appreciate Your patience with me *HaShem*. You have watched over me even when I was undeserving, and You have saved me countless times. No one in the world could ever care for me as much as You do. When I stumble, You are there to lift me up. When I rise up, You are there to grasp me in Your light. Without You *HaShem*, I am nothing.

Tefilla For Simplicity

HaShem, You appreciate even the simplest acts of man and thereby return a reward to him. Your mercy is unending. How can I thank You for the good You bestow on me?

We are taught it is not the complicated acts that You seek, but rather those performed with a realness of heart. There is nothing like a simple Jew who completes a *mitzvah* with love. I want to love You with a simple love. Please show me the way to reach true devotion. Guide me on the path to simple, wholesome love.

Help me to see myself as in a mirror, to know how to correct my deeds. Draw me close to You, *HaShem*. All I want is to come close to You. "Bless me with love, grace, loving-kindness and mercy in Your eyes and the eyes of all who see me." (Prayers From the Heart pg. 422)

HaShem, what a pleasure it is to be a drop in the ocean, part of the people you call *Klal Yisrael*. Thank You for giving me the *mitzvos* and the privilege of being your servant. Please send me *mitzvos* I can perform with love, so I can give back to you whatever is in my ability.

Tefilla for Hisbodidus

HaShem I love You so much. The *Torah* You have given is so precious and dear to me. When it's cold outside I still feel Your warmth. As much as darkness manifests itself in the night, there is so much light from the mercy You shine on me.

Every day when I wake up I'm created anew. Unfortunately, I don't feel very new. This is not Your fault, *HaShem*, as I am the one who takes little time to reflect on the things that I should. This is why I need to start a regimen of *hisbodidus* into my schedule.

HaShem, I try to do *hisbodidus*, but it seems like the channels to Heaven are blocked for me. This is only a mirage – a false vision from my imagination – but, being mere dust and ashes, I lose hope and lose patience with my prayers. I am begging You for help, *HaShem*. I know the gates are open for me, though I choose to ignore them. Help me set aside a proper time for *hisbodidus* and during those times please hold open the gates of Heaven and help me pour out my heart to You.

Assist me, *HaShem*, to say the right things once I start speaking, to pray for all my spiritual and physical needs without confusion as to what my real needs are. Help me to confess all my sins of today and mistakes of the past. Let my ego be nullified as I stand before You, pleading to be forgiven and drawn closer to you. Let me not forget the needs of others during my prayers. *HaShem*. You give me so much hope and joy and I feel so loved. Aid me please in expressing my true love and feelings for Your commandments. Don't allow days and weeks to pass with my plate remaining empty. Thank You, *HaShem*, for teaching me about *hisbodidus*. For this alone I'm indebted to You.

Tefilla Tikkun Chatzos

Thank You, *HaShem*, for giving us the *Torah* and commandments. How do I begin *HaShem*, to speak to You about how much we need the Temple to be rebuilt in this generation? There is so much bloodshed, anti-Semitism, immorality, crime, hunger, loneliness and sadness in the world. My self-confidence is shattered just thinking about how much has to be done to bring perfection to a world so full of confusion. I have learned that there is a special prayer, unlike any other, that can help bring an end for all of us to this long and bitter exile.

Unfortunately, this is a difficult devotion to practice successfully; it entails waking up in the middle of the night when I am already tired out from my work and studies. *HaShem*, I understand how important this practice is and I want to incorporate it into my life as the great *tzaddikim* of old used to do, but I need a full *yeshua* (salvation) in order to do so. I need help to control my *yetzer hara*, which does not want to let me rise at this precious hour of *avodas HaShem*. Also, I need support from my family such that they too understand the importance of this *avodah*.

When I'm successful in rising at this hour, please help me to use my time wisely by saying the *Tikkun Chatzos* prayer, repenting, doing *hisbodidus* and learning *Torah*. Help me please, *HaShem*, to remain awake often from *chatzos* until the morning sunrise, learning *Torah* with tremendous enthusiasm. By my practice, let the evil in the world lose strength and be diminished.

Saying the *tikkun* is good, *HaShem*, but to say it with all my heart, how precious it will be in Your eyes. Help me to understand a little bit of our true loss at this hour and truly feel our present exile. Let the remembrance of the *Bais Hamikdash's* destruction be real in my heart. Help me feel shame over my sins, my ancestors' and the sins of our nation. May my prayers at this hour be so heartfelt that my eyes come to tears! After having expressed and felt the destruction of our Temple, please help me return to joy at the thought of the imminent redemption, as otherwise my heart would not be able to contain its anguish.

HaShem, please help me to not let this propitious hour slip by. Dovid HaMelech never slept past this hour as he took control over his time and life. I want to do the same and serve You righteously, never forgetting that there is a *Shechinah* in exile waiting for me to bring her home. Help me *HaShem* to know and never forget that I too can make a difference by arising for *chatzos*. Thank You, *HaShem* for opening the gates to my prayers as You have done so often. There may be millions of prayers entering the gates of Heaven; nonetheless You don't turn my words away but rather welcome them.

Tefilla for Kavanah

Even though I am dust and ashes compared to You, *HaShem*, You still find time to hear my supplications. Though millions of Jews are seeking You, You listen and welcome everyone's prayers. Many of us praise You but all the praise in the world falls short, as no being can comprehend what You do for them every second.

Praying is an easy action; all I have to do is open my mouth. To open my heart, though, to truly pray to You, that is something much higher. It is something I need to work on constantly as my prayers are said usually by rote, without concentration. *HaShem*, please help to make my prayers pleasing before You, to make them true and real from the depths of my heart.

When attacked by outside thoughts during prayer, help me cast them aside, elevating them back to their source above. Help me to not be discouraged when my prayers seem not to be answered the way I want. Help me realize that You are the one who truly knows what is best for me.

Assist me *HaShem* in praying with humility and negating myself. Help me during prayers to always remember my fellow Jews, who are also suffering, and the pains of the Divine Presence. Let my prayer instill in me *emunah* and a true change in my character. Help me make a proper balance between *Torah* study and prayer.

HaShem, without You I am nothing. You give sustenance even to the lowest beasts. I am a Jew and my *neshamah* is holy. Help me draw close to You through prayer and have the feeling of wholeness of soul. Thank You for all the love You give me, all the hope You bestow on me, and for giving me the ability to communicate to You.

Tefilla for Shabbos

Shabbos is the greatest gift in the world, *HaShem*. It is so holy, so precious. Thank You for giving us this special day when our soul shines double. No other nation has *Shabbos* but ours. What a present You have blessed us with!

Help me to rest and have peace of mind on *Shabbos*. May I be a vessel to take in all the *kedusha* that *Shabbos* has to offer to my soul! Let the excitement of *Shabbos* be appreciated by my family and those around me. Help me to prepare something each day of the week in preparation for the coming *Shabbos*.

HaShem, please assist me to not be careless with my speech and actions on *Shabbos*. I want to make the most of this special day to grow spiritually, drawing closer to You. Open my heart and eyes that I should see the *kedusha* of *Shabbos* and not be held back by remembering weekday thoughts.

Preparing *Shabbos* for myself is good but help me to give it to others as well. *HaShem*, I want to have guests for *Shabbos*, but the burdens of extra preparations are difficult. Please ease my burden so that I can give *Shabbos* to other people. Help me also to participate in hearing the *Torah* portion and other community activities in honor of this precious day.

Thank You, *HaShem*, for this beautiful day of blessing. All our sustenance comes from the three meals and prayers on the *Shabbos*. Therefore, may the *seudos* I make, or participate in, be of wholeness and tranquility.

Rebbono Shel Olam, what would I do without the holiness of *Shabbos* in my life? Thank You for this wonderful and important day of rest. That is, a day to reflect and appreciate all that You have given me. May I keep and observe its laws in the most respectful way.

Tefilla for Ahavas Yisrael

Ribbono Shel Olam, no being can ever comprehend the *chesed* You do every moment for Your creations. I am just one of the many whom You have treated with an enormous amount of mercy. For this, I am truly grateful.

I want to imitate this *midah* of kindliness that You possess, *HaShem*, to the best of my ability. I want performance of *chesed* to be a natural part of my being, so that I do so without even thinking. Not only this, *HaShem*, but I want to literally crave doing *mitzvos* of this kind.

Master of the world, let me not fall into the trap of judging others negatively, whether it be my spouse, friend, or a stranger. Help me to see only the good in others. Help me to see the subtle contrasts, not just in black and white. All Jews are important and there is a spark of holiness in each one of us. Please open my eyes and heart to this.

Thank You once again *HaShem* for encouraging us to love our fellow man. There is nothing in the world more important to me than to serve You righteously. Even though I am not worthy, You have treated me with so much love and understanding.

Prayer for Kavanos Halev

Thank you, *HaShem*, for allowing me, a simple Jew, to speak to You about the troubles of my heart. *HaShem*, I am so distracted by the things of this world that sometimes I forget there is a Creator controlling all the events of my life. I'm so busy with work and daily chores that there is little time to meditate on the purpose of the world. If only I could feel Your nearness, it would mean so much to me and fix all of my anxieties.

I know the sages have told us that we can elevate even our sleep to a level of true devotion to *HaShem*, but this is something I feel far from. It's almost as if it's so easy to become close to You that I push You away instead. Help me, *HaShem*, to turn my life around and bring it more realness. Enable me to connect my every action to You in complete sincerity.

Everywhere I look, I am able to see Your glory, though I seem to forget to connect my surroundings to You as I should. When I finally take notice, there are times when I still lack the concentration and devotion I should have in being Your servant. Please help me to appreciate the things I have been blessed with, those things I have overlooked and all the happenings of my life. Allow me to reflect before performing the *mitzvos*, giving them the proper *kavanah* of my heart.

Thank You, *HaShem*, for all the patience You have shown me all these years of my life. Thank You for all the times that I was far from You and, nonetheless, You drew me near to You even though I was unworthy. Allow me to complete my soul and to spread the wisdom of our sages to all mankind.

Prayers Written in Later Years

It is interesting for the reader to see the transition in the thoughts of the author as he grew throughout the years. In the next section of the book, "Prayers written in later years," the reader can really feel the closeness with *HaShem* - earlier it's like a faint voice crying out in the darkness. It is taught in the Talmud that after certain periods of life, the plateau of forty years of age, a person is given more clarity and wisdom. The difference between the early prayers and the later prayers proves that a person should be patient and never give up. I wrote this work while hoping that you, the reader, will persist and eventually find clarity in your own personal meditations to *HaShem*.

Advice

HaShem, rather than leave us alone throughout life, You have left us Your blueprint for the creation of the world, the *Torah*, to guide us through all obstacles. Not only this, but You have also given us sages to lead us through the trials of life, so we do not have to travel them alone. For this alone, *HaShem*, I give You praise.

As simple as it should be to ask for advice and connect to leaders of the generation, I haven't had the privilege to get so close to the sages. In fact, many of my questions go unanswered as I seem to fear even asking them. As far as finding the right answers inside the *Torah*, my lack of knowledge makes this difficult.

So here I am *HaShem*, lost in this world of confusion without the guidance I truly need. Therefore, I ask of You, *HaShem*, to lead me in the right pathways. Help reveal the right answers to me, so I don't make further mistakes in my life.

Please also help me understand the *Torah* in more practical ways so that all my answers should always be there for me. Guide me in finding the sages who can understand my soul root, so I won't feel endlessly alone.

Thank You *HaShem*, for Your availability towards me so that even when all else fails, You're always here to guide me.

Anger

HaShem Yisborach, I understand how You can overlook my many sins, but to overlook my anger and frustration is remarkable. You know, the only reason a person is angry is because they are selfish and prideful. Yet even when I have these forbidden emotions You still sustain me with Your patience, because You are slow to anger Yourself.

So, what do I do? I am frustrated with my life that things don't go as I plan. I know I must get rid of the anger I am feeling but it isn't something I can just turn off.

Chazal say that if a person has anger, the *Shechinah* leaves him. *HaShem*, if You don't want anything to do with me during this time, I have no one who cares as You do. Please don't leave me and please help me to calm myself down.

Thank You, *HaShem* for having the patience to deal with me.

Bris – The Covenant

HaShem, the Covenant between You and Your nation Israel is unbreakable. It is the most cherished relationship we have together. Thank You for giving us the holy ability to have a *bris milah* and to be able to serve you in purity, free of sin, free of any flaws.

What do I say to my Father in Heaven, when I break this Covenant? It not only causes harm to my soul, but also to all other Jews since we are one nation. What can I do? Something as simple as being pure with one's eyes and heart seems impossible at times.

If only I feared You enough that I wouldn't sin; oh, how close I would be to You, *HaShem,* and to the *Torah.* My entire life would open up; I would be a free man! But instead I am trapped by the prongs of evil, and I don't even know why. Going after vanity never provides any real satisfaction and, quite frankly, I know better than this. So, what can I do to improve my ways?

I pray to You *HaShem* that You help me overcome all obstacles and tendencies which draw me further from You. Open my heart to the *Torah* and a pure and healthy way of life.

Thank You, *HaShem* for your continued patience with me. Even though our Covenant together has been flawed by my many mistakes, I am taking this time to reconnect to You, *Hashem,* and to begin anew.

Calmness of Mind

HaShem, You have blessed us that we are not alone in this world. Whatever happens to us, You're in complete control and oversee everything so that events should go easier for us. I don't have to worry that I'm alone in my suffering or trials, as I know that You are there supporting me through everything.

Even knowing this, I still find myself confused. Sometimes I can't even make a simple decision. Thoughts linger in my mind and eat away at me endlessly. I can become so confused that I keep talking endlessly about my problems. I want to have positivity, yet I keep thinking about all the things that could go wrong. I'm aware that this isn't the way; that I should have, at the very least, a simple faith in You, *HaShem*. Please *HaShem*, help me to not allow my life to be dictated by confusions, as this can become one of the worst sufferings in my life. Help me to be confident and to make only the right choices always. Be there for me; give me peace of mind and tranquility in my life. Let there always be peace around me among family, friends and acquaintances. Please don't allow thoughts to overtake my peace of mind.

Thank You, *HaShem* for Your compassion towards your creatures, for allowing me to overcome this trial, and to serve You with a calm mind.

Children

HaShem, You are our Father in Heaven and You understand how difficult the role of a parent is. When we, Your children do something wrong, You try to lead us on a better path. You're slow to anger, compassionate, and a great teacher as well.

HaShem, I want to be like You and be an unbelievable parent and role model. I want to provide the best teachers, guides, study partners and friends for my children. Our generation suffers so many failures when it comes to education. We as parents make so many mistakes and forget to focus on our children's important qualities. We are many times too negative to them and don't praise them enough for the good they accomplish.

You know, it's not easy being a parent. Please guide me in all aspects of parenthood. Help me to have *nachas* from my children. Lead me to find the best health care and schools, and to nurture their every need.

Parenthood is the greatest blessing given to us, to leave behind a legacy of our name and very blood. Thank You for this opportunity to raise children in the ways of the *Torah*. Thank You for giving me a Jewish wife and children to bless the Name of *HaShem* throughout the world.

Confession

HaShem, I stand before You in embarrassment because there is nothing hidden from You. You already know all my sins before I confess them and have probably pardoned most of them, yet I am still too ashamed before You to confess my wrongs.

A king of flesh and blood would have already punished me for my actions, yet the one and only *Melech* has exhibited the utmost patience with me. Thank You for this.

So, what am I to do? It is so difficult to speak to You, *HaShem*, even though You already know everything about me. I'm just so embarrassed as I feel I have disappointed You to the utmost extent.

Well, here I am standing before You, rattling about how difficult it is to say what is in my heart, when You have already showed Your compassion towards me; otherwise I wouldn't even be here with this opportunity to amend my wrongs.

HaShem, please forgive me for my sins done purposely and accidentally. *Chazal* say that our prayers take the place of the *karbonos*, so please let this prayer be seen as a replacement for the appropriate *karbon* relative to my sin. Please wipe my slate clean and allow me to start over with joy in my *avodas HaShem*.

I did do the following mistakes…. (List them…)

Thank you, *HaShem* for overseeing my life with compassion. For always being there even after I messed up and for giving me this new opportunity to start over with the *Shechinah* beside me.

Controversy and Strife

HaShem Yisborach, everywhere around me seems to be controversy and strife between people. The only shelter from this storm seems to be in Your arms, coming to You and finding shelter. Thank You for always giving me a place to run to, to find comfort and know that someone cares.

HaShem, my enemies seem to look at me as someone to take advantage of and abuse. Why I have become their target, I have no idea. Maybe I stood out above others as someone easy for them to hold hostage with their evil plans?

It is to You, *HaShem* that I cry out for compassion. Let the evil ways of others not overtake my composure and peace of mind. It is literally all I have left. They have taken so much from me, but please don't allow them to take my heart and mind.

I understand that these people are powerless against me and it was because You wished me to exert myself in my faith that I've gone through these trials. *Hashem*, You got me! You won! I am coming to You for help and I seek You now at all times. Please defend the honor of Your simple servant and bring justice on those seeking my harm. Bring me the compassion that I seek and complete peace of mind. Thank You for always being there for me, unlike my friends who see my pains and look the other way.

Death

HaShem, I don't know why it is necessary to exert the strength of the *Satan* to take a person out of this world. For me, my life is a taste of death already. I am so far from You, I sometimes feel all alone. The *Shechinah* has left me due to my many sins; I myself am responsible for Her leaving.

Chazal tell us that being poor is an aspect of death. I am constantly struggling with my faith when it comes to money issues. I never seem to have all of my needs and I lack the financial freedom to feel alive. But I have learned that money doesn't buy happiness; rather it is family and the satisfaction of giving to others that brings us real life.

HaShem, I feel as if each day I am drowning in my sorrows and there is nobody to help me. Please send me the gift of life, the gift of freedom from worry and anxieties. Help me to feel alive again both physically and spiritually.

You, who hears our prayers, thank You for hearing my pleas and for giving me a new breath of life this moment to find life, happiness and hope for the future.

Desire and Yearning

There is only One *HaShem*, Maker of Heaven and Earth. It is to You I call in my times of trouble and You are there to sustain me. You attempt to draw me close even when I am far and confused. Thank You, *HaShem* for Your continual kindness to my soul.

HaShem, I yearn to be closer to You. My soul is a completely pure and holy entity that You created. Its only desire is to attach to the highest source. However, being attached to the physical body, the mind must overcome many barriers to be near to You, *HaShem*. Help me to be persistent; through performance of the *mitzvos* with joy, assist me in shedding all obstacles that separate me from You. Lead me in the pathway of *lishmah*, that everything I do should be completely for Your sake without reward.

My soul yearns for You, *HaShem*. Help me to channel this yearning through the gates of Heaven and be near to You. Thank you for connecting me to my soul root and helping me overcome the *yetzer hara* that wanted to separate us. Please draw light from *Eden* into my soul and let me shine while attached to Your holiness. Let the light of the *tzaddikim* radiate into my soul; let the holy light of all the Jewish nation penetrate and help me be a source of blessing to the world.

Eating

I was thinking, why must we eat food? The angels, which can't even reach the highest level of soul as we can, do not require physical food, so why do we?

To take anything physical and refine it, like gold or diamonds, makes it even more precious. Here we are in this world, refining our bodies and souls so that they should be perfect. Perfection can only come when there is first imperfection.

The refining process is what draws me near to You, *HaShem*. Thank You for not treating me as an angel or a heathen, but as a Jew that can go from unpolished to polished.

Help me to say the blessings before and after eating with absolute *kavanah*. Assist me in saying the words properly, slowly and with concentration on their true meaning. Help me to add the many *kavanos* to elevate the food to the highest level. May I elevate all the sparks as intended! I ask You, *HaShem*, to send me the holiest sparks through the portions I eat, sparks of souls and *kedusha* that will elevate my soul above its current level. Let the sparks then provide me with physical and spiritual strength to do many *mitzvos lishmah*.

Please provide me with *parnasa* and food for the next day so that I should lack nothing. Bless me endlessly through the sparks of the food that I should maintain complete attachment to You at all times. Thank You, *HaShem*, for sustaining me both physically and spiritually, with all of my needs.

D'vekus, Enthusiasm and Fervor

"He is your praise and He is your G-d." (*Devarim* 10:21) You know *HaShem*, I was wondering why it is that we start all prayers with thanksgiving and praise.

I understand now that it is the praising of *HaShem* and being thankful for all that we have that brings us to levels of *d'vekus*. We can't call to You and serve You with fervor if we don't appreciate what we've already been given. When we do, this lights up our souls to pray properly.

Therefore, thank You, *HaShem* for all the kindness You have bestowed on me. From the moment I awaken each day until I retire at night, You are there leading me and encouraging me to live a good life. Throughout the day, You put me in positions that test my loyalty towards Your commandments; You also constantly set up opportunities that are an advantage for me. Help me to find you in all happenings and awaken my heart to serve You with excitement and positivity. Remind me when I perform commandments not to do them as a routine, but rather out of my great love for You.

HaShem, serving You is no burden on me. I accept upon myself all the commandments with love. Thank You, *Hashem* for the opportunities You have given me.

Eyes – The Power of Sight

What a gift You have given us, *HaShem*. We have the ability to see and live with sight. Not only this, but You have also given us the ability to see millions of colors, depth of field, and more. Through sight, our other senses function with more agility. Thank You for this wonderful blessing.

Whenever there is something we are blessed with, we also have the ability to take advantage of this item and use it for good or for bad. How insulting it must be when we take for granted our blessings. Help me to use my eyes only for performing *mitzvos* and connecting to You, *HaShem*. Help me to elevate all of creation to its proper place in the *Sefiros*. Help me to be worthy of this unbelievable miracle of eyesight.

Sometimes items come into my field of vision that lack holiness. Instead of bringing me down to negativity and impurity, help me to turn the other way and not look at things that don't draw me closer to You. Let my life be one of value and importance.

HaShem, please help me that my eyesight should always be healthy. Besides physically seeing your wonders, help me to also see spiritual visions of Your greatness. Thank You so much for this miracle and may I cherish it all the days of my life.

Faith

When all is said and done, all a person has left is his faith. *HaShem*, I want to be the most faithful person. I want to be near to You and trust that You are protecting me at all times.

We know everything that happens is for the best, but it is not always easy to keep our faith strong when things go in ways that are difficult. Hardships are there to lead us closer to You, but sometimes we use them to push You away instead. Thank You for Your patience and for believing in me.

Help me to grow in my *emunah* and not to question Your ways. Let me connect to You at all times and therefore live the life of the World to come, Where I will know in my heart that You are there, and everything is for the good.

I would like to be an inspiration to others as well. Help me to spread faith in Your Oneness throughout the world. Allow me to be a walking *sefer Torah* and to make a *kiddush HaShem* wherever I travel. Thank you, *HaShem* for the opportunity to serve You and believe in the *emes* of Your *Torah*.

Festivals

HaShem, thank You for giving us holy festivals to rejoice in Your kindness and exaltedness. What a wonderful opportunity we have to recharge ourselves in our *avodas HaShem* through the *mitzvos* of festivals.

This joy we have in the festival carries over into a positive month for us. Therefore, I ask of You, *HaShem* that You assist me in thinking positive thoughts during this festival. Help me to rejoice with family and friends for the holiness of the festival in ways that draws us near to Your Oneness. Assist me in performing all the *mitzvos* of the festival with the utmost scrutiny, *kavanah* and joy. Through this, may I rectify all my wrongdoings and fix up the past.

Many people waste away their festival in relaxation, laziness and *bitul Torah*. They think that a festival just means long meals and laughter. They don't realize that every moment of the festival has meaning and can accomplish remarkable things for their soul. I ask of You, *HaShem*, that I should use the festival wisely; that my soul be elevated thereby; that I should study a tremendous amount of *Torah* and meditate on it continuously. Help me to be elevated through the holy prayers of the festival that my prayers should open the gates and be beautiful before You.

Thank You, *HaShem* for hearing my prayer and drawing me close to You. There are no words to express my thanks to You for giving me these holy days to reconnect to You and the *Torah*. Thank You.

Healing

HaShem, it is You who hears our prayers and truly heals the world. For every illness, there is a healing, but it is You, *HaShem*, who must lead me to the right medicine. Please be gracious on me and grant my request to be strong and healthy.

HaShem, I stand before You as a broken body and soul. I need healing so much and yet I look to doctors, medicines, even the great *rabbis*, only to find myself still suffering. I know everything has a time and I might still need to be ill a bit longer before you release me from this Divine test; however, I ask, if that is the case, that You help me to cope better with the sickness. Help me have the strength of mind to see through it and not give up hope. Bring on me the holy *Shechinah* so that if I have to suffer, at least I won't be alone or feel depressed.

I understand that the main reason a person suffers is that he needs to repent or that his soul needs to reconnect to You. Therefore, I should just do my best and be happy that You noticed me, that I now have an opportunity to fix myself. However, that being said, I am calling out to You, *HaShem* to heal me quickly nonetheless; I declare my faults before You, *HaShem*; please now open the gates of healing and help me get out of this state of weakness as soon as possible. I simply can't serve You and make a new beginning when I am plagued with so many physical and emotional obstacles. Therefore, release me from this hold and I will serve You with all my heart.

Thank You, *HaShem* for hearing my pleas, for allowing me to speak to You, and for granting me the *Shechinah* to be by my side through this illness. May I be healed soon, *Amen*.

Honor and Pride

HaShem, I don't know why it is that I keep pursuing honor and dignity amongst my peers. The only honor I should be obsessed with is the honor of *HaShem*. This very concept of lowering oneself from pride can be learned from Your *midos, HaShem*.

You are completely selfless, creating a world just to share Your light with Your creations. Unfortunately, when I create or make anything, my first thought is to show it off to others so that I can feel proud of myself. When You created the world, every intricate detail in nature and all of creation, Your thought was only that others should benefit.

Please help me, *HaShem* to exert my energies in this world only to bring honor to You and to lift up others. Help me to live a life of *lishmah*, doing the *mitzvos* for Your sake. If this leads me to positions of greatness, then so be it, but I only want what is best to help the Jewish people and elevate the world. Help me to not run after high positions to raise myself above my fellow. Actually, help me to avoid such things, unless they are necessary for the good of my brethren.

Thank You, *HaShem* for overlooking my desire for pride. A proud person has no *HaShem*; he just has himself. Help me to be completely pure in my intentions and please continue to lead me on a good path. Thank You for saving me so many times from high positions, which would not have led me closer to You.

Humility

It is so easy to be humble; I just have to look at the ways of *HaShem*, and I can know how to live properly. Humility is one of *Hashem*'s greatest *midos*. In fact, the entire world was created with humility and *HaShem's* greatness is revealed daily.

So why is it *HaShem* that I struggle so much with this character trait? It is something that should come easier than other traits, as it is something that affects me constantly.

While I do something wrong, You sustain me with Your humility and still give me life. You overlook my many improper and negative thoughts as well. Constantly, You pile up more and more humility as You continue to sustain me through my ups and downs. Yet, why do You do this?

It is because humility is one of the greatest character traits. With humility comes an endless amount of kindness and sweetness to mankind. So, I must learn from You, *HaShem,* how to be humble.

Please help me to care for all of creation and to love my fellow Jew more than myself. Help me to stay away from pride, which is a very evil character trait. Assist me in giving of myself to my family, friends and even strangers. The more I grow in wisdom, help me to also see my lowness compared to You and the world. Help me to realize that all my accomplishments were simply my job as a servant to his Master. There is no reason for me to feel pride from doing just what I have been commanded and instructed.

Help me not to look at others as if they are lower than I am; that I am greater for my accomplishments than they are. Rather, let me see myself as a tool that can be used to lift others up, not because I am greater but because I have been blessed from above to receive all that I have.

Thank you, *HaShem* for Your patience, for overlooking the study and *mitzvos* that I did *shelo-lishmah* and considering them as *lishmah* anyways. Your humility towards me, only I know; You and I are the only ones entitled to the secrets of my every moment. Please continue to reveal to me Your kindness and blessings.

Land of Israel

HaShem, you could have given us any land in the entire world, but instead you gave us Your richest and most beautiful home, a place destined for greatness to house your only establishment, the Temple. Thank You for thinking of us as a special nation worthy of these benefits. Especially, I thank You for thinking of me as worthy to be a Jew.

There are so many extra *mitzvos* that can be done only in the holy land. Many of them can only be done after *Mashiach's* arrival. Not only do we need the final redemption to perform more commandments, but also to rebuild Your holy Temple.

Today we are worthy that many of our nation are able to dwell in *Eretz Yisrael*, and those who aren't able can easily travel to visit our precious land. Even so, we haven't truly returned to our land, but will soon with the arrival of *Mashiach*. For some, the easy access to *Eretz Yisrael* has led them to take its holiness for granted. They might sin in the land as if it were just like any other place in the world, not appreciating its inherent *kedusha*.

I too fall into this trap. Yes, I try to do as many *mitzvos* as I can in the holy land, but I still take it for granted. The holiness of the place has slowly lost the special feeling it once had. Please help me return to You and to the *kavod* of *eretz hakodesh*. Help me to own land and a house in *Eretz Yisrael* so that I should grow more attached to it. Assist me in supporting many Jews in Israel so they should fulfill many *mitzvos* here in my merit. Help me to be a part of *Toras Eretz Yisrael* and to enable many scholars to learn *Torah* there. May I be a part of the rebuilding of Jerusalem and inspire the righteous *Mashiach's* arrival in our time. Thank You again *HaShem* for this precious gift that You have given us. May we both dwell and settle in *Eretz Yisrael* with a final peace and tranquility.

Life and Longevity

HaShem, You gave us the gift of life. It is something we many times take for granted and don't appreciate. Yes, we may have our ups and downs, our trials and tribulations, but that too is a gift. Thank You, *HaShem* for the opportunity to serve You and to live a life that is true.

You know people can complain about many experiences and difficulties that they face regularly. They can even say that some events in their life are more than just hard but are clearly tests from *HaShem* to see if they will hang in there with their faith, not losing hope when everything else seems to be falling apart. But that is just it; everything else may seem to collapse but *HaShem*, You are always still there, waiting for me to reach out.

HaShem, I ask of You to make my life one of worthiness. Help me to always be happy with my lot and to find joy even in the most confusing times. It is not just a long and healthy life that I pray for, but also one that has mostly genuine moments. Please bless me that I should live a good life, filled with *Torah* and *mitzvos*. Help me to not waste time oversleeping, doing mindless things and not appreciating the moments. Bring me a life of peace because living through controversy isn't genuine.

Thank You, *HaShem* for this precious gift. May I cherish every moment to serve You and to grow in *Yiddishkeit*.

Love

HaShem You are full of so much love for Your creations. Constantly Your love is outpouring and endless for me. Just when I think You are fed up with me to an extent I can no longer fix, Your love for me overrides Your judgmental side. Thank You for such an outpouring of love and patience.

This love and kindness that You have *HaShem*; I want this character trait too, to love my fellow with so much compassion. Certainly more, I wish to love You, *HaShem*. So today, I start anew with a more generous outlook towards being kind and loving. Obviously, there must be some balance, so people don't take advantage, so please help me to have also just enough *Gevurah*.

As much as I take comfort in Your love for me, *HaShem*, I must also feel love from others around me. I need this in order to thrive and serve You. Therefore, please surround me with genuine loving people who are close to You. Keep me away from those who have hate in their heart and are up to no good. Help me to give of myself to those who will appreciate me.

HaShem, may Your mercy fill the entire world. Thank You for all Your love and compassion. May I henceforth return this love full-fledged.

Shalom Bayis

HaShem, chazal teach us that through *shalom bayis* one has blessing in his life. When a person gets married, the two become whole and complete. Through this, they are able to perfect their souls through raising children.

I am blessed to have found my life partner; however, we differ on so many aspects of life. While I have many strengths, I also have a lot of weaknesses. The same thing with my spouse because of these differences, we are sometimes at each other's throats. Our home, instead of being one of peace, becomes one of tension and strife. What can I do *HaShem*? It isn't as if I am not trying my best to unify with my partner and make peace, but emotions seem to get in the way, sometimes even anger, and there is no longer any tranquility.

So, I am sitting here wondering what I am to do. I will just apologize and ask for forgiveness from my partner, but it won't change things. Therefore, I ask You to send me down Your holiness, the *Shechinah*, into my home to fix things. Bring me a lasting peace with my spouse. Let us not walk around at odds with each other but as true partners in the service of *HaShem*.

Thank You so much *HaShem* for this blessed partner in my life, for being able to share life with someone, the joys and the obstacles, but not being at it all alone as I once was. Please bless us with *parnasa*, which is a common reason for lack of *shalom bayis*. Bless us with *nachas* from our children and show us a beautiful future together, a loving peace.

Melody and Song

There is nothing in the world that can touch a person's heart like music. What a wonderful gift you have given us to awaken our heart and to bring us to joy. When nothing else can rouse our heart to Your commandments, it is music that can touch us in a very special way, drawing us closer to You. Thank You, *HaShem* for this precious gift.

You know there are many types of music. There is music that is clearly descending from holiness and then there is music that is really not so good. This music that isn't so good, it has a temporary effect on us; it might make us dance, sing or be happy but it doesn't last. In fact, it is only our good deeds that protect us from it drawing us into deep sadness.

Please I ask You, *HaShem*, help me to use music to draw closer to You. Help me to meditate on the *nigun* till it opens all the gates in Heaven for me. This is what the prophets did to draw closer to You. They used the music as a repetitive meditation to refocus their energies for good. Please open up the holiness of *nigunim* for me so that it should have such a positive effect on me too. May I compose many beautiful songs and utilize my musical talents to draw people closer to *HaShem*!

May I be blessed to hear songs of the angels above as they sing their praises to You. Please help my prayers to be like music before You, *HaShem*, and may I play sweetly before you as our holy King David once did and still does from the Garden of Eden.

HaShem, please open my heart to Your commandments. Let me be a true and complete vessel before You. Thank You for blessing me with a tune, and may I present my life before you as not just a song but rather a symphony of good deeds.

Messiah

Each of us internalize the concept of *Mashiach* in our own way. Some people don't take the idea of *Mashiach* seriously enough, while others will resort to strange and lengthy methods to draw him closer. I don't think there is just one way to think about *Mashiach*; however, the most basic foundation is the idea of awaiting his arrival every day, to believe in the concept of *Mashiach* and the idea that there is always hope.

How great a gift is it, this idea of continuous hope in the future, no matter what. This idea of hope doesn't move; it's always there for the taking. So, I ask You now, *HaShem* to bring the righteous *Mashiach* soon in our times. See our readiness that tells us we can't live without a Temple to serve You in. Look down upon us and see Your wayfarer just sitting here and waiting to be nearer to You. Therefore, open the gate of salvation, send down the third Temple and bring us the final redemption.

I'm sure You know, *HaShem*, that we have been waiting for a long time. Too long, I am sure You know. There are so many *mitzvos* we can't perform without prior redemption. Our adversaries sit around mocking us all day, referring to us as a defeated nation. Why should this continue, when You eagerly desire the redemption as well? Therefore, *HaShem*, join me in my prayers, in my *avodah*, and hear, act and redeem us NOW.

Mikvah

The holy *mikvah* is more than just a body of water where we immerse ourselves; it is a tool and blessing that You have given us that enables us to start over, that helps us draw closer to You and reconnect to the original holiness we had at the time of birth. It is something quite amazing and not really from this world.

I ask of You, *HaShem* to open up the holiest and purest channels above through my *mikvah* immersion, enabling me to return in complete *teshuva* and purity. Help me to refine my ways through this simple immersion and become completely reconnected spiritually.

As I dunk in the water, let me leave behind my mistakes and take a new step forward on a pathway nearer to You. This body of water is only a vehicle towards finding You, but it is You, *HaShem*, who purifies a person. All *mikvaos* truly are connected with water from *Eden*, but the naive one screams out, "water, water." This is because at the River from *Eden*, the *mikvah* really isn't about physicality. It is *mamash* so much more.

Please *HaShem*, help me to have very holy meditations as I immerse in the waters. Let me leave behind my connections to *gashmius*, those evil desires and sins that plague me all day; allow me to enter this pure world of closeness to my Creator. Open up the gates that my thoughts and intentions in the *mikvah* should lead me to new revelations in *Torah*. Let me not immerse according to habit, but rather in total sincerity, returning to my Maker. Thank You for creating something so beautiful as the *mikvah*. I am grateful to have a *mikvah* that I can visit to perform this holy act. May my ways from now on be holy and let the *mikvah* protect me throughout the day and the week thereafter.

Money

HaShem, how naive I have been in thinking that the world is truly controlled by money, that power comes from this materialistic craving. You know, we think that money opens all the doors for us in life; but really, it hasn't any true power except to confuse people. Thank You, *HaShem* for saving me from this bottomless pit of desires. *Chazal* say that a person dies with only half of his dreams of financial freedom.

So, what is this financial freedom everyone chases his entire life? I have seen so many people destroy their entire life over money issues, thinking that they are in control of their finances when really, they aren't. *HaShem* giveth and *HaShem* taketh away. Money is constantly changing hands and revolving. It isn't meant to sit on someone's lap and be used exclusively. Rather, money is a gift to continuously keep moving and sharing.

Please help me to never let my finances or business dealings take control of my mind. Help me to put *Torah* and *Yiddishkeit* first in my life, before business and money. Allow me to acquire true financial security, which stems from true faith in *HaShem*. Please make sure I never become ill over money nor let it control me. Therefore, I also ask that this *tikkun* not be something that comes with hardship either. Please always make sure my family has enough food, money for utilities, and other living expenses.

Without my really noticing it, You have always cared for me on a daily basis. I have always had food to eat and a roof over my head. Thank You so much for this. Please also bless me with good real estate investments that don't distract me from learning *Torah*. Help me to have business dealings only with *HaShem*-fearing individuals. Please, most of all, bless me that *Torah* should be in the forefront of my life. Thank You again for always providing for me. Please bless me with food and everything my family needs, today, this week, this month, and this year. Thank You.

Overcoming Obstacles

If there were no obstacles to overcome, there could be no feeling of reward and satisfaction. The key to overcoming obstacles is to go on the offensive instead of taking a defensive stance. Therefore, help me to not ignore the things I must overcome, but to rather attack them and move forward past them.

HaShem, I have so much on my plate when it comes to things that need to get done. The bills just pile up and there isn't enough time get everything done. I wish for a relaxing life, so I slowly get things done, yet there seems to be no end to it all. Without You, *HaShem*, I know things could be much worse. Please help me to catch up on everything I need to accomplish.

I could endlessly be on the phone calling companies, teachers and business partners, but I am more than this. Please help these difficult moments pass by without incident. On top of all this, I am dealing with anxieties about everything. The physical items are enough of a test, but I also have to deal with my emotions running wild, and this can lead me to depression and sin. Please help me get control of my life and make things easier than they have been. I don't say this as a complaint, but rather a plea to help me persevere through the storms of life. I know, *HaShem*, the only reason You created all of these troubles was, so I would pray to You for salvation. Well here I am, praying with all my heart. Please grant me peace of mind and happiness. Please just make everything be okay. I cast my burdens and worries upon You, *HaShem*. If You will only make things better for me, I would appreciate it from the bottom of my heart. Please remember that I am only flesh and blood. I can only accomplish so much each day and I have enough distractions in my life. Have mercy on me; answer me on the day I call and give me all of my needs.

Peace

HaShem, is there peace in the heavens? I am told that up above, it is all peace and *shalom*. Down here it's not. It's a world of confusion and chaos. I am not saying this to complain, *chas v'shalom*, but we *mamash* need Your help. I know You hear prayers, especially those asking for peace. What would *Gan-Eden* be like; what would the upper worlds be without *shalom*? *HaShem*, I want to taste this serenity down here on Earth, in my life as well. I am sick of all the controversy that surrounds me. It scares me and devastates me. Everyone seems to be looking for conflict, as if life is boring without it. I want no part of these fights. It hurts me to see others fighting. Please surround me with peaceful neighbors, friends and associates.

Besides this, inner peace is even more important. Please help me to make peace between my *midos* and my physical body, which seems out of balance, and my emotional health. *HaShem*, it is You who gives healing and balance; I beg You for this. For a life of happiness, stress free, with a good support system of family and friends. These are the basic needs of every person to keep a healthy outlook in his life.

I really believe in keeping a life of *shalom*. I have been doing my best to surround myself with peace, but it seems impossible, almost as if hostility seems to follow me. I sit here talking to you without any inner peace or sanctity for my soul. Rather, I am filled with anger, strife, confusion, and loneliness. Seeing this, the *Shechinah* has left me and I can't bear it. Please save me and shine the light of peace on me.

Thank You, *HaShem* for hearing my prayers and for answering me on this most important topic. I can only try, but I need Your help to remove this impurity from my surroundings and heart.

Physical Desires

HaShem, as much as we are troubled by controlling our physical desires, we are thankful for them. Without this opportunity to control ourselves through free will, we could never really appreciate true good.

Each of us has his personal tests when it comes to these aspects; however, most of us follow some of the same patterns of desire. That of sexual purity seems to be the most troubling for most of us. The others seem to be money, fame, pride, and food.

Without getting into the practical details of these desires, I would like to pray generally for salvation from all physical desires. Help me to realize my true purpose in life and to connect more spiritually to You. Assist me to stay more focused on holy things and let those fill the void inside me. Always I am looking to satisfy my emptiness with more emptiness. It really makes little sense, as materialistic things never quench real thirst.

So, I ask of You, *HaShem*, to help me rise above the normalcy of the world, which is to give into *tyvos*. Help me to not dwell on the things I don't have, and to appreciate what I do have. Allow me to transform myself from an individual craving physicality to someone worthy of the *Shechinah*.

Thank You, *HaShem* for all the good You have done for me, for Your patience as I went after worthless desires. Thank You for giving me a chance to fix these wrongs and redirect my heart to purity.

Praise

How can I praise You, *HaShem*, when Your praise is infinite? Any attempt at thanking You would only be insufficient. There are so many miracles You do for me that I don't even know about, and those I am aware of are too many to recall. So, how do I praise You?

Maybe this is Your praise, the concept of recognizing that we can't sufficiently praise You, and reciting this to You is the greatest praise itself? *HaShem*, I understand that the angels are constantly singing praises before You in the heavens. *Chazal* teach us that the angels cannot reach the elevated levels we can actually attain. This is because we have free will and, if we do praise You, it is something we do with a complete heart. We actually choose to praise You, while they simply have no choice.

Therefore, *HaShem*, I stand here now choosing to praise You with an insufficient palate. I choose anyway to try because I understand how much You love when the angels, mankind, animals, and even insects call out to You in song.

HaShem, I thank You for the amazing life You have given me, for this tool of a body with 248 limbs and 365 sinews to perform *mitzvos* with. For a month, to attempt to praise You three times a day with words of prayer and appreciation. Thank You, *HaShem* for this wonderful opportunity.

Repentance

HaShem, maybe the greatest gift You have given us is the ability to turn back the clock on our deeds and repent before You. It is actually quite amazing, this so-called "free pass" You have given us (by many times overlooking our first sins). Well I know I shouldn't look at it as such; that would warrant my not taking sins seriously, but my point is that You are so slow to anger and so compassionate to us, that You overlook so many mistakes that we do.

Maybe it is recognizing this that will help me to also be free of sin, because of my love for You, and not just because I am afraid of retribution. So here I am, my Father in Heaven, full of sin and deceit against You, yet I can still speak to You as a friend and ask You to help me eliminate all my blemishes.

Please *HaShem*, whether it is through sincere repentance or Your forgiving mercy, please take away any suffering normally decreed for sins such as mine. Lead me on the path of righteousness and integrity. Fix me, purify me and open the gates of purity before me. Let me live a proper, healthy physical and spiritual life.

I know You have heard this all before that I am sorry and will never be sinful again. I'm aware that You are tired of my repetitious sins. I am genuinely sorry for all these shameful acts. Thank You for bearing with me through the good times and the tough times.

Shame

HaShem, thank You for believing in me even during times I don't believe in myself. It is a great support for me to know, feel, and see how much You strengthen me. I really can't begin to count all the blessings You have given me.

I stand here today feeling so much shame. I'm constantly messing up in *halachos*, *yiras HaShem* and simple life tasks. What is worse is that I know I can do better, but my self-esteem is too low to be motivated toward Your service. So here I am, full of anguish, guilt and shame. Will I come out of it myself? Probably eventually, but I would rather be lifted up by Your holiness now because time is being lost that could otherwise be used to serve You, *HaShem*.

Please therefore, lift me out of this state of mind and bring me to one of nearness to You, a mind-state full of happiness and tranquility, knowing that my repentance has been accepted. Thank You, *HaShem* for making *teshuvah* possible, for sustaining me through my ups and downs. Thank You for being my Master, King, Father in Heaven and most of all, my friend.

Simplicity

HaShem, in a complicated world, there is one thing, which is simple: that is, to believe there is one *HaShem*. Sometimes we complicate our lives so much that we miss the simple meaning of life itself. Performing the *mitzvos* with absolute simplicity can sometimes be greater than stringencies and thought-out actions. Thank You for making the *Torah* and *mitzvos* so beautiful and yet so simple that any of us can perform them.

So here I am *HaShem*, lost in my stringencies, needless anxieties and stresses. I've made some *mitzvos* so complicated that I don't even enjoy them any longer. Please help me to once again enjoy the beauty of just performing a *mitzvah* with joy and for the simple sake of the *mitzvah* itself. Help me to elevate the *Shechinah* and thereby fix the world as well as my own imperfections. Allow me to ride this *mitzvah* to the greatest of heights and to connect to You with complete humility.

Thank You, *HaShem* for allowing me to pray to You, for opening doors of opportunity in my life, and allowing me to find You in all things. Please return me to *avodas HaShem* performed *lishmah*.

Sleep

The Talmud teaches us that a good portion of our life is spent sleeping. Now if my sleep habits were normal, maybe I could still appreciate this concept of sleep rejuvenation; but I fail miserably at getting a good night's rest. It is quite remarkable that You created man that he requires sleep in order to live. Even the great sages, who forego most of their sleep, still required some in order to live. It is as if You wanted us to never to waste time, and yet understood that we must be given some time in order to recuperate from performing the commandments. Thank You, *HaShem* so much for thinking of us in this regard. If it wasn't for sleep, we wouldn't be able to make that new beginning when we awake. Serving You afresh and brand new in the morning is really a wonderful experience.

HaShem, I am not getting the most I could out of sleep. I have crazy insomnia. So much time I waste just tossing and turning in bed, wondering, praying how I am to function the next day with a lack of sleep. Then, when I finally do fall asleep, I get woken up or have a restless night, not benefiting from REM sleep as I should. The next day, I feel fatigue and my mind isn't at full capacity to work and study. I wake up sometimes as if I am literally being woken from the dead. It simply takes me too long to get going in the morning after such a difficult sleep. Instead of gaining strength through sleep, I seem to be losing far more from these bad sleep habits.

Please help me *HaShem* to keep a good sleep schedule. Remove all insomnia and restlessness from my sleep. Please turn these hours of sleep into a *mitzvah* through the intention that I am going to sleep only in order to be stronger in my *avodas HaShem*. Through this, may my sleep be a gem in my life instead of a troubling phenomenon. Thank You so much for giving us this opportunity to do a *mitzvah* through sleeping. May I have helpful, pure and relaxing dreams! Help me to say the *kriyas shema al hamita* with the proper intentions and not to be lazy with *negel vasser*. Thank You again for all Your kindness and the ability to serve You anew.

Suffering

HaShem, thank You for minimizing my suffering. Some people suffer tremendous bitterness every day of their lives, but even though I have many trials both physically and spiritually, I still bask in the knowledge of Your Oneness.

I recognize this and spread Your greatness around the world, please have further *rachmanus* on me and release me from all hardships. While others seem to live a normal life, I find myself constantly confronted with obstacles that take my strength away.

HaShem, I know in life that everyone must experience vicissitudes. I only ask of You, *HaShem* that my downs should still have tremendous positive energy inside to allow me to lift myself up again.

Please *HaShem*, understand that I am coming to You during this time of trouble. I could run away to material distractions instead, but rather I am praying to You to fill my emptiness with light. Please fix all the things that have suddenly gone wrong for me and make them into a right that I can understand. I feel alone in this darkness, even though I have come to You to pray. I just can't bear a lengthy suffering when I can hardly manage my simple life as it was before. Please, be with me through these trials and let me only suffer minimally, so that I hardly notice the retribution. I know that is a harsh word to use, 'retribution', but I only mean well with the words of this prayer. All I want is to find salvation in You.

HaShem, You have always been slow to anger with me, overlooking almost all my misdeeds. During this time of suffering I turn to You first, before doctors, friends, and others. Please make my *mazal* turn around for good tidings. Thank You again for hearing my pleas.

Tefillin

HaShem, do You realize how much I love the *mitzvah* of *tefillin*? If I could wear my *tefillin* to sleep, I would do so just to have these holy boxes resting upon my head. The parchments, they shine inside my body and soul. I feel as if I am transformed into a world of only sunshine and light.

It isn't enough though, *HaShem*; I want to perfect this *mitzvah* in all aspects. The blessing over *tefillin*, I want to say it with perfectly pure intentions. I want to draw down light into my soul that it should radiate inside me all throughout the day.

Please *HaShem*, help me to fulfill this *mitzvah* properly. Help me to draw near to You in purity, transform me from this materialistic world to a world of only light. *Chazal* say that wearing the *tefillin* is like performing all of the *mitzvos*, so great is the light of the *parshios*. Please open my heart through this *mitzvah* and let me be a completely new person. Thank You so much, *HaShem*, for sharing this *mitzvah* with Your servant. The Talmud says that every day, You too wear a spiritual pair of *tefillin*. As I perform this *mitzvah*, I bind myself to Your pair of *tefillin* as well. May every turn of the straps around my arm draw down light from the corresponding *Sefiros*. Please allow the holy light from the name *Shakai* protect and inspire me this day. Bring down *shefa* into my life and my heart that I should have a day filled with *chein*, gracefulness, basking in the light of the *Torah*. Please allow the fire of the *Torah* and the parchments to reach into my soul, igniting it so that my *avodas HaShem* is done completely *lishmah*.

In these holy boxes is light that is trapped and has difficultly coming out because of my unfortunate sins. Please release this light and help me to get the full experience from this *mitzvah*. Allow the light to flow through the holy letters of *shin* etched on my holy *batim*. Let the holiness be an amazing experience, opening up the prayers and *Torah* studies I recite while wearing them. Give me complete clarity about my life and my purpose. Shelter me with the shadows of the *Shechinah*. Guide me and lead me on a good path, a healthy pathway. *HaShem*, I am so excited to share this *mitzvah* with You. Thank You!

Controlling Thoughts

HaShem, I am so blessed to have a brain with which to comprehend the *Torah* and the world. Thank You for giving me this special gift to use and to cherish.

I understand from *chazal* that my thoughts are very important. I'm responsible for them and negative thoughts can lead one to commit sins, *HaShem* forbid. I also understand that we must call out to You constantly, asking for help with our thoughts. While any thought can be controlled by simply switching topics, it isn't so easy in practicality.

So here I am, *HaShem*, my thoughts rambling out of control. I am trying to take them by the reins in order to control them, yet I see I also need Your assistance. Please help me to place my thoughts in order. Allow me to function normally, without confusions and stress. Bless me with nearness to my Creator and with a life that is stress-free. Thank You, *HaShem* for this wonderful gift. Please help me that my emotions should not take control of my thoughts. Remove all thoughts of anger from my heart and bring my mind to peacefulness. *HaShem*, I really do cherish Your assistance; please therefore, fill my mind with Your holy Names to guide me. Protect me from all evil and any negative temptations. My mind is sometimes my biggest battleground. I feel as if something in my brain is off and not functioning at full capacity. *HaShem*, please join me in controlling my thoughts and bring me to new levels of purity. Thank You for Your kindness, for hearing the prayers of Your servant in need and answering me on the day I call.

Traveling

HaShem, it is amazing that You gave mankind the ability to walk and travel from place to place. As technology grows, traveling becomes easier and easier. Though it is so convenient, it is quite easy to forget You during our excursions. Therefore, I pray that You send the *Shechinah* with me in my travels, that She should guide and protect me from all harm.

Help me to properly understand how to connect to You in my home so I can know how to journey with the *Torah* as well. This is why it mentions first in the *Shema* prayer that we should study *Torah* at home, and then only later it says to study as we go along the way. We must first learn to connect to the *Torah* while stationary, only then will we know how to while out in the world.

HaShem, please assist me in staying holy during my travels. Help me to protect my eyes and heart from all negative thoughts. Assist me in going from place to place, successful and well liked. May I complete everything with grace, connected to the *Shechinah* at all times! Thank You, *HaShem* for allowing me to make blessings and thereby sanctify Your holy Name in many places as I travel. Help me only to make a *kiddush HaShem* and to find favor in the eyes of all the people I speak with. Bless me that my travels should be safe and that I should accomplish everything I set out to complete. Thank You for being with me for good.

Truth

HaShem, You created the world with truth and justice. Thank You for bringing truth into the world. It seems so rare today to find truthful people and proper guidance.

All I want in life is to find complete truth in my heart, to serve You with absolute pureness and for the sake of sanctifying Your holy Name. Why truth has to be so hard to come by, I have no idea. It is almost as if it were something hidden among the righteous. For most of us, it might even take a lifetime to find the complete truth, so misguided are we when we follow the masses instead of furthering our personal growth. We spend our life stumbling over addictions, materialism, and honor; for what? These things only draw us further from the truth of the *Torah.*

HaShem, please protect me from the evil in the world. Help me to see with a clear picture where I am really holding. Let my eyes be open, realizing the best *rebbe, rabbi, rav, chavrusa,* and friends for me to surround myself with. I keep falling into bad traps through connecting myself to people who don't live their life in order to find the truth. Help me to also believe that the truth is in the *Torah,* as it is called the *Torah* of truth (*Toras emes*). This is because *HaShem* is the G-d of truth. Thank You, *HaShem* for this wonderful goal of finding the absolute truth while in this world. My journey has only just begun in finding the total truth.

Understanding

HaShem, thank You for giving me the understanding to realize the true meaning of life. When it really comes down to it, understanding is really the true goal for everyone. Having the ability to understand something helps a person to accept a situation. Therefore, one realizes that everything that happens can only be for good because HaShem only does good.

Please bless me with *yishuv hada'as* so I should be able to go through life with clarity. If a person doesn't have clarity, really, he shouldn't move from his place. How can a person walk even one step if he is not connected to *da'as*? Without the *Shechinah* in one's life, there is only emptiness and false gain. Therefore, HaShem, I beg you to give me the clear vision to see through all the obstacles that confront me and to have the *da'as* to persevere through them.

HaShem, help me to simplify my life so I don't ignore the portions of Judaism that are foundational to serving You. Restore my *da'as* so that everything I do should be calculated properly and performed with the utmost perfection restore the happiness that has left my heart. Let this be a new beginning for me in *avodas HaShem*, one where the *Torah* comes first, an *avodas HaShem* that leads to complete *lishmah*. Thank You, HaShem for creating *da'as* and free will so we can properly find You, through our search for truth.

The Greatness of Prayer

88: It is written, "Cast your burden upon *HaShem*, and He will sustain you." (Psalms 55:23)

89: If a human being has a patron and goes to him once, he is received. The second time he is also received, but the third time, he is refused an audience. By the fourth time, no attention is paid to him at all.

90: This is not true of *HaShem*. No matter how many times you bother Him, He receives you. (Midrash Tehillim 5:6)

91: Rabbi Eleazar said: "Prayer is greater than good deeds. No one had done more good deeds than Moses, but still, he was only answered after he prayed." (Talmud Berachos 32b).

92: When I pray, I'm getting out of the natural order of the world. I'm even getting out of the order of the *Torah*. Imagine, *HaShem* forbid, somebody is sick. According to the order of the world, this person has to die. And I'm praying, "*Ribbono Shel Olam*, can you please change all the orders of the world?" Imagine I did everything wrong in my life; according to the orders of the *Torah*, I'm the lowest person, and I'm praying, "*Ribbono Shel Olam*, please fix my soul." Praying is that I'm in an absolute infinite world.

A complete person is somebody who knows exactly when to be in order and when to be beyond order.

Imagine you don't say any words; you just cry. Prayer has no beginning and no end. Praying is something... something else.

King David says "*v'ani tfilati*" [I am a prayer]. The question is, are you a prayer? Are you filled with prayer? If you're filled with prayers, it means you're beyond nature because then I can see a person who's the lowest person, and I believe that this person can be lifted up to the highest level.

Reb Nachman says, everybody knows that Israel is the headquarters for miracles, because your level of miracles depends on how much you are connected to prayer. If a person tells you, "I don't believe in miracles", do you know what that means? That this person has never prayed in his life.

Israel is the headquarters of praying, the headquarters of miracles, and the headquarters of believing completely in our relationship to *HaShem*. So, what is it to be in exile? We don't know how to pray, because the holy Temple is the headquarters for praying. Israel is the land of prayers, and the holy Temple is the headquarters.

As long as I'm not connected to that 'fixing', I still think certain things I can do and certain things I cannot do; I can go only so far.

The moment I'm really on the level of a little bit fixed, *mamash* I'm infinite, infinite.

Praying means I'm standing face to face with *HaShem,* and I can do anything in the world. I'm connected. I'm plugged in to the real electricity (Reb Shlomo Carlebach's Teachings, page 44).

93: The Hebrew word *hitpalel* [meaning prayer] is actually the reflexive (*hitpael*) form of a verb, meaning "to judge". Therefore, it denotes judging oneself, or coming to a correct opinion of oneself, or at least an inner attempt to accomplish this. In other words, [prayer] is an attempt to gain true judgment of oneself.

Prayer denotes a step out of active life, so as to gain a true judgment about oneself. It is an attempt to gain true knowledge about his relationship to *HaShem* and the world. It strives to infuse one's mind and heart with the power of judgment in such a manner as to direct the mind and heart to an active life that is purified, strengthened and sublime.

The process of arousing such self-judgment is called *tefillah*. In the vernacular, we speak of this as prayer, but that word is an incomplete expression of the concept. "Prayer" denotes asking for something, but this is only a minor aspect of *tefillah* (Rabbi Shimshon Raphael Hirsch Horeb 618).

94: If our prayers were not *tefillah*... working on our inner selves to bring them to heights of recognizing the truth and to resolutions for serving *HaShem,* then there would be no sense in fixed times and prescribed forms for them. But our prescribed prayers are not facts and truths of which we are already conscious; they are concepts we wish to awaken and renew in ourselves. The less one may feel inclined to recite a prayer, the more necessary it may be to say it (Rabbi Shimshon Raphael Hirsch, Commentary on Genesis 20:7).

95: Prayer is to the soul what food is to the body (Sha'shuim 1).

96: The essence of prayer is the joy of loving *HaShem* (Sefer Chassidim 90, 87).

97: The pious man waits an hour before praying and concentrates his thoughts upon *HaShem* (Berachos 30b).

98: Unless we believe that *HaShem* renews creation every day, our prayers grow habitual and tedious (The Baal Shem Tov).

99: Gold and silver are purified through fire. If you feel no improvement after praying, either you are made of base metal, or your prayer lacked heat (The Korestser Rebbe).

Prayers of the Heart

100: Do not hurry when you leave a place of worship (Rabbi Yosef Karo, Shulchan Aruch).

101: I love to pray at sunrise, before the world becomes polluted with vanity and hatred (The Koretser Rebbe).

102: The main purpose of prayer is to break down one's haughtiness so that he returns to *HaShem* (The Vilna Gaon).

103: The man who persists in knocking will succeed in entering (Moshe Ibn Ezra).

104: HaShem proclaims, "Make an opening for me no wider than a needle's eye and I will open for you a gate through which armies can pass (Shir Hashirim Rabbah 5:3).

105: He who prays for his neighbor will be heard for himself (Bava Kama 92a).

106: R' Chama b. R' Chaninah said: "If a man sees that he prays and is not answered he should pray again, as it says: "Wait (hope) for *HaShem*, be strong and let your heart take courage and wait (hope) for *HaShem*" (Berachos 32b).

107: When Chizkiah Hamelech, in his illness, heard the announcement of Yishayah in the name of *HaShem* that he was to die, he replied, "We have a family tradition from David, that even if a sharp sword is resting at a man's throat, he should not refrain from pleading mercy." Thereupon he prayed and was granted fifteen more years of life (Yishayah 38:1-5). R' Yochanan and R' Eleazar quoted regarding that incident, "Though He may slay me, yet will I trust in Him" (Iyov 13:15) (Berachos 10a).

108: "To love *HaShem* your *HaShem* and to serve Him with all your heart." With your heart means prayer. Pray with love and *HaShem* will love your supplications, as R' Zeira explained: A man may have a loving friend, but as soon as he asks a favor of him or needs his help, he turns to be his enemy and rebuffs him. But *HaShem* loves a man better the more he begs, invokes and prays. He even suggests man to pray to Him, as it is said, "Call unto Me and I will answer you" (Shochar Tov 4).

109: Even though man is immersed in darkness and far from the light in his natural physical state, he is still permitted to stand before *HaShem* and call Him by His Name. Man is thus able to temporarily elevate himself from his lowly natural state to exist in a state of closeness to *HaShem* and cast his burden upon Him. This, one can do through prayer (R' Moshe Chaim Luzzato – Derech Hashem).

110: R' Elazar used to give a coin to a poor man and only thereafter prayed because he said, it is written, "I, in *tzedaka*, shall behold Your face" (Bava Basra 10a).

111: R' Yose b. Chaninah would pray in the morning at sunrise so that he might have upon him the fear of Heaven the entire day (Yerushalmi Brachos 4).

112: Every lock has a key. The locks on the gates of prayer are also opened by keys. Happy is he who can find the right key to every lock. However, even he who does not know how to find the proper key that fits should not despair, but instead he should learn from the thief. Just as the thief breaks the lock whenever he does not have the key, so too a man must break his heart with humbleness in order to penetrate the gates of prayer (Yalkut Sippurim).

113: When Rabbi Akivah prayed, it was with such fervor that a man could leave him in one corner and find him later in another (Berachos 31a).

114: When one sits in the synagogue, *HaShem* stands above him, for it is said, "The Eternal stands in the congregation of *HaShem*" (Berachos 6a).

115: *HaShem* asks, "Is there anyone who attended the synagogue and did not find My Presence there?" (Devarim Rabbah 7)

116: If a man sees that he has prayed without answer, he should continue praying (Berachos 32a).

117: Pray and pray again. There will come an hour when thy request will be granted (Devarim Rabbah 2:12).

118: There are times when a person experiences such ecstasy that words of praise and song form automatically on his lips. When one is worthy of this ecstasy, it is a sign that his sins have been forgiven. The Hebrew word for song is therefore "*shira*", related to the word "*hashreh*" meaning "to rest." It is a sign that the Divine Presence rests on the person composing the song (Yalkut Me'am Lo'ez).

119: Prayer is a powerful factor, for it reverses Divine decrees (Bereishis Rabbah 71).

120: A person must not despair of mercy (cease to pray), until his last breath... even if a sharp sword is resting upon his neck (Yalkut Koheles 989).

121: The nature of man is that, when he is bothered by someone, he can make up excuses to slip away. But the Holy One, blessed be he, no matter how much you bother Him with requests, will never make up reasons to excuse Himself from listening to your earnest pleas. He will receive you at all times (Jerusalem Talmud Berachos 9:1).

122: All gates are sometimes closed, except the gates of prayer of those wronged by men, for it says, (Amos 7:3) "Behold *HaShem* stands on the wall of '*anach*' (oppression)."

Prayers of the Heart

123: From the time of the destruction of the *Bais Hamikdash* the heavenly gates of prayer have been closed. But when one is aggravated to the point of crying for Divine help, his prayer is answered (Bava Metzia 59a).

124: *HaShem's* Name 'Rachum' (merciful), expresses the idea that even when a man must be punished, if he merely calls out to *HaShem* for mercy, *HaShem* will reduce the intensity of his suffering. (The power of prayer is great indeed!) (Sforno Shemos 34:6)

125: If a man faces east and wishes to pray to *HaShem* for wisdom, he should turn his face a little towards the south, for the brain is towards the right. If he wishes to pray for riches, he should turn towards the north, for understanding is in the heart which is at the left (Zohar 3: 257b).

126: A prayer never loses its value (Jerusalem Talmud Berachos 1:2b).

127: If what you have hoped for comes to pass, it is well; if not, hope again (Tanchuma B'shallach 12).

128: A man should pray that he be safeguarded against misfortune before it is at hand (Sanhedrin 44a).

129: One should rise early and be counted among the first ten [in the *minyan*], for even if one hundred people come after him, he is given as substantial a reward as all of the hundred people combined (Berachos 47b).

130: He who strengthens himself (makes a strong effort for prayer), has no adversaries (Sanhedrin 44b).

131: Prepare your heart and then pray, as it is stated, "If you have prepared your heart, spread out your hands to Him" (Iyov 11:13).

132: There is nothing in the world that is closer to *HaShem* than the heart of man. It is dearer than sacrifice and more precious than all the treasures of the world combined (Zohar Chadash; Rus Rabbah 80a).

133: How long must a man remain in prayer? Until he (his heart) is faint (Midrash Tehillim 31:3).

134: Divine inspiration can be attained through deep meditation in prayer (Tur, Orach Chaim 98).

135: "Once, R. Chanina ben Dosa, while standing and praying, was bitten by a poisonous lizard, but did not interrupt his prayers. His disciples asked him, 'Our *rabbi*, did you not feel anything? He answered, "I take an oath. Because my heart was intent on my prayer, I felt nothing" (Jerusalem Talmud Berachos 5:1).

136: And he should not grind out a blessing as though it came from a machine (Berachos 47a).

137: "With his mouth and lips he gave Me honor, but his heart was far from Me" (It is important to pray with thought) (Yishayah 29:13).

138: He who makes his prayer a fixed chore, is unable to plead and supplicate for compassion (Berachos 28b).

139: "Let not your prayer be a matter of fixed routine, but rather a heartfelt supplication for mercy and compassion, before the Divine footstool of the holy One, blessed be He" (Pirkei Avos 2:18).

140: Be careful to pray the *Shema* and *Shemoneh Esrei* (on time and with proper concentration) (Pirkei Avos 2:18).

141: Whoever reads the *Krias Shema* with its two-hundred and forty-eight words, with proper concentration, will merit that *HaShem* will watch over all of his two-hundred and forty-eight organs (Tanchuma Kedoshim 6).

142: One who says the prayer should say all of it with his heart and soul and if he cannot concentrate on all of it, he should concentrate at least on one of the eighteen supplications. One which one? On the first one [Avos] (Berachos 34b).

143: The prayer of the pious is short (Mechilta B'Shallach Vayass'a 1).

144: Anyone who stays long in prayer is assured that his supplication is not returned empty-handed. But hasn't it been said: "Anyone who stays long in prayer and speculates on it comes to sickness of heart?" There is no contradiction. Here we are referring to one who stays long and speculates on it (expecting its fulfillment as a reward for his lengthy prayer); and here is one who stays long but does not speculate, saying: "Hope in *HaShem*; be strong and strengthen your heart, and continue to hope in *HaShem*." (Tehillim 27:14) (Berachos 32b).

145: Man, in his prayer should always include himself in the community (pray for all people in the same condition) (Berachos 29b).

146: The Holy One, blessed be He, yearns for the prayers of the righteous. Therefore, He restrains (detains and causes to delay) the salvation of the *tzaddikim* and advances the salvation of the wicked (Bereshis Rabbah 68:5, Pesikta Zutrasi *29:18).*

Excerpts from Sefer Hamidos by Rebbe Nachman

147: One who prays in a *synagogue*, it is as if he brings a pure meal offering.

148: The holy One, blessed be He, is found in the synagogue.

149: One who has a humble opinion of himself, his prayer is not despised.

Prayers of the Heart

150: The prayer of another is more effective than one's own prayer, and even a *tzaddik* needs the prayers of others.

151: Anyone who engages in *Torah*, the holy One, blessed be He, fulfills his needs.

152: A person should not beseech excessively for anything. Even though we find in various places high recommendation to pray at length for something (see the introduction to Outpouring of the Soul and chapter 6), one should not be obstinate and demanding, but full of hope and prayer that the holy Merciful One G-d bestow on him, even more, goodness and blessing as only He knows what is best).

153: On a rainy day, salvation flourishes in the world, and advocates of merit enter before Him [G-d].

154: The prayer of an individual is not heard unless he concentrates in his heart, but the prayer of a congregation is heard, even though all of them do not [pray with] a full heart.

155: It is a *mitzvah* for one to have respectable clothing at the time of prayer.

156: They instituted blessings [to G-d] in this world, so that [people] should become accustomed [to saying them] in the world to come.

157: Through prayer, one can change the fortunes (set by the constellations).

158: Through having trust, the holy One, blessed be He, hears one's prayers.

159: Before the prayer, give charity, and bind yourself to the *tzaddikim* of the generation (this is done with a verbal disclosure, "I hereby bind myself to all the true *tzadikim* of the generation.")

160: When a congregation prays, it is a time of [Divine] favor.

161: One who has [access to] a *synagogue*, and does not enter there to pray, causes his children to be exiled.

162: For everything -- whether for something big or for something small -- you should pray.

163: Come early and stay late in the *synagogue*, for this is how you will lengthen your life.

164: One who has the ability to beseech mercy for his friend, and does not beseech, is called a (inadvertent) sinner.

165: Prayer is greater than virtuous deeds and sacrifices.

166: Through giving charity with two hands, one's prayer is heard.

167: *Shabbos* and *Rosh Chodesh* (the first of the Jewish month) are conducive (*segulas*) to raise up prayers.

168: When you are not at peace with the world, your prayer is not accepted.

169: You should pray for the peace of the city in which you live.

170: Someone who prays joyfully, the holy One, blessed be He, honors him and punishes his oppressors.

171: One who increases the merit of Israel (especially where circumstances would seemingly deem them culpable), through this, he arouses salvation, and the salvation comes through his hand.

172: One who does not pray concerning the suffering of Israel is called a (inadvertent) sinner.

173: A person needs to pray for his offspring, and for all those who will come after him.

174: Someone who prays for the sake of Israel, the holy One, blessed be He, atones for all his sins.

175: A sick person who prays for himself with tears, the holy One, blessed be He, will certainly heal him and accept his prayers.

176: When you want to uplift your prayer, pray for the sake of Israel.

177: Through having trust (in G-d), a person's prayer is heard.

178: Someone who is humble is able to cry out in his prayer from the heart.

179: Through joy, your prayer will come into the palace (chamber) of the King.

180: One who derives no pleasure from his prayer, should pray with glad song.

181: One who prays with intensity, the holy One, blessed be He, hears his prayer.

182: One who took a vow upon himself, his prayer is not accepted until he fulfills his vow.

183: One who makes the *tzaddik* happy, his prayer is heard.

184: Before praying, one should attach one's spirit to the Creator, and due to the attachment, the words will emerge from his mouth of their own accord.

185: When you hear yourself being humiliated and you are silent, you merit that the holy One, blessed be He, will answer your request.

186: One who prays for his friend, through this the holy One, blessed be He, doubles for him the good he [receives].

187: One who prays about the destruction of the Temple, through this, he will merit praying with heart and body.

188: Prayer done with joy is pleasing and sweet to *Hashem*, may He be blessed.

Prayers of the Heart

189: One who has humility -- even when he prays [only] in thought, the holy One, blessed be He, fulfills his thought.

190: One who requests mercy for the members of his generation merits revelation of the Divine Presence.

191: Through songs and praises, one draws down the Divine Presence.

192: One who fulfills [the maxim] "Your fellow man's money should be as dear to you as your own," through this he merits praying with heartfelt intention.

193: There are prayers that are not accepted above until one gives the amount of charity equal to the number of letters in the prayer relevant to the matter. For example, when one prays with the words, "Give me children," one needs to give charity according to the number of the letters in the words "Give me children." The number of the levels probably means the *gematria*- numerical value -- in the example given this would be 592; in Hebrew letters this would spell out the word - you give the set amount.

194: There are times when one person's prayers for salvation are not enough; [help] will only come when a number of people pray for it.

End Excerpts

195: If you set your prayers to a pleasant melody that you enjoy, you will pray with more devotion, and your feelings will be aroused by the words you utter. When you petition *HaShem* for something, select a melody that puts you in a prayerful mood. When you sing His praises, choose a melody that evokes happiness, so that your mouth brims with love and joy for Him who knows your thoughts, and you will praise Him with deep ardor and jubilation (*Sefer Chassidim*, 32 (158)).

196: A short prayer said with concentration is preferable to a long prayer said without concentration (Tur Orach Chaim 1:4).

197: It is better to exalt *HaShem* with just a few praises that are said slowly and reflectively, rather than hastily rushing through a large number of praises.

The Orchestra that performs before royalty always plays at a slow tempo. Surely, when singing *HaShem*'s praises, we should do likewise. Indeed, the *Levites* in the *Bais Hamikdash* used to chant their hymns very slowly (Sefer Chassidim 35 (315)).

198: If a book falls on the floor in front of you while you are praying, and because of that you cannot focus your thoughts on your prayer, you should pick up the book and continue to pray with concentration. Before picking up the book you should finish the *berachah* you started, and you should keep in

116

mind the place where you will continue. However, if you are praying with total concentration, you should not pick up the book, because he who prays with concentration will enter the World to Come (Midrash Tanchuma, Tzav 7) (Sefer Chassidim 42 (777)).

Ana Bekoach

אבג יתץ	צְרוּרָה tzerurah	תַּתִּיר tatir	יְמִינְךָ yeminecha	גְּדֻלַּת g'dulat	בְּכֹחַ b'koach	אָנָּא ana	חסד Chesed	1
קרע שטן	נוֹרָא nora	טַהֲרֵנוּ taharenu	שַׂגְּבֵנוּ sagvenu	עַמְּךָ amecha	רִנַּת rinat	קַבֵּל kabel	גבורה Gevurah	2
נגד - יכש	שָׁמְרֵם shamrem	כְּבָבַת k'vavat	יִחוּדְךָ yichudecha	דּוֹרְשֵׁי dorshei	גִּבּוֹר gibor	נָא na	תפארת Tiferet	3
בטר צתג	גָּמְלֵם gamlem	תָּמִיד tamid	צִדְקָתְךָ tzidkatecha	רַחֲמֵי rachamei	טַהֲרֵם taharem	בָּרְכֵם barchem	נצח Netzach	4
וזקב טנע	עֲדָתֶךָ adatecha	נַהֵל nahel	טוּבְךָ tuvcha	בְּרוֹב b'rov	קָדוֹשׁ kadosh	חֲסִין chasin	הוד Hod	5
יגל פזק	קְדוּשָׁתֶךָ kdushatecha	זוֹכְרֵי zochrei	פְּנֵה p'neh	לְעַמְּךָ l'am'ach	גֵּאֶה ge'eh	יָחִיד yachid	יסוד Yesod	6
שקו צית	תַּעֲלוּמוֹת ta'alumot	יוֹדֵעַ yodeh	צַעֲקָתֵנוּ tza'akatenu	וּשְׁמַע ush'ma	קַבֵּל kabel	שַׁוְעָתֵנוּ sha'vatenu	מלכות Malchut	7

| וָעֶד: va'ed | לְעוֹלָם le'olam | מַלְכוּתוֹ, malchuto | כְּבוֹד kevod | שֵׁם shem | בָּרוּךְ baruch | (בלחש) (silently) |

Tikkun HaKlali

Psalms Chapter 16

א מִכְתָּם לְדָוִד: שָׁמְרֵנִי אֵל, כִּי-חָסִיתִי בָךְ.	1 A verse frequented by *Dovid*. Watch over me Almighty since I take refuge in You.
ב אָמַרְתְּ לַיהוָה, אֲדֹנָי אָתָּה; טוֹבָתִי, בַּל-עָלֶיךָ.	2 I said to myself concerning G-d, "You are my Ruler, the good I receive is not your requirement to me."
ג לִקְדוֹשִׁים, אֲשֶׁר-בָּאָרֶץ הֵמָּה; וְאַדִּירֵי, כָּל-חֶפְצִי-בָם.	3 On account of the righteous ones of yore, and the mighty ones, I am granted all my needs.
ד יִרְבּוּ עַצְּבוֹתָם, אַחֵר מָהָרוּ: בַּל-אַסִּיךְ נִסְכֵּיהֶם מִדָּם; וּבַל-אֶשָּׂא אֶת-שְׁמוֹתָם, עַל-שְׂפָתָי.	4 Let the grief of idolaters increase, I will not pour their blood-libations, nor mention the names of their G-Ds.
ה יְהוָה, מְנָת-חֶלְקִי וְכוֹסִי-- אַתָּה, תּוֹמִיךְ גּוֹרָלִי.	5 G-d is my assigned share and portion, You guide my fate.
ו חֲבָלִים נָפְלוּ-לִי, בַּנְּעִמִים; אַף-נַחֲלָת, שָׁפְרָה עָלָי.	6 The lines are fallen unto me in pleasant places; yea, I have a goodly heritage.
ז אֲבָרֵךְ--אֶת-יְהוָה, אֲשֶׁר יְעָצָנִי; אַף-לֵילוֹת, יִסְּרוּנִי כִלְיוֹתָי.	7 I bless G-d who has advised me, during the nights as well my conscious admonishes me.
ח שִׁוִּיתִי יְהוָה לְנֶגְדִּי תָמִיד: כִּי מִימִינִי, בַּל-אֶמּוֹט.	8 I always place G-d before me, for He is at my side, so I do not stumble.
ט לָכֵן, שָׂמַח לִבִּי--וַיָּגֶל כְּבוֹדִי; אַף-בְּשָׂרִי, יִשְׁכֹּן לָבֶטַח.	9 Therefore my heart is glad, and my glory rejoices; my flesh also dwelleth in safety;

י כִּי, לֹא-תַעֲזֹב נַפְשִׁי לִשְׁאוֹל; לֹא-תִתֵּן חֲסִידְךָ, לִרְאוֹת שָׁחַת	10 For Thou wilt not abandon my soul to the nether-world; neither wilt Thou suffer Thy G-dly one to see the pit.
יא תּוֹדִיעֵנִי, אֹרַח חַיִּים: שֹׂבַע שְׂמָחוֹת, אֶת-פָּנֶיךָ; נְעִמוֹת בִּימִינְךָ נֶצַח.	11 You will teach me the path of life, and give me satisfying joy in Your presence, Your right-hand offers endless delight.

Psalms Chapter 32

א לְדָוִד, מַשְׂכִּיל: אַשְׁרֵי נְשׂוּי-פֶּשַׁע; כְּסוּי חֲטָאָה.	1. An enlightening song of *Dovid*. Fortunate is one whose misdeed is forgiven, whose sin is covered up.
ב אַשְׁרֵי אָדָם--לֹא יַחְשֹׁב יְהוָה לוֹ עָוֹן; וְאֵין בְּרוּחוֹ רְמִיָּה.	2. Fortunate is the man whom G-d does not perceive in him any wrongdoing, and there is no trickery in his spirit.
ג כִּי-הֶחֱרַשְׁתִּי, בָּלוּ עֲצָמָי-- בְּשַׁאֲגָתִי, כָּל-הַיּוֹם.	3. Because I was silent my bones withered, from my groaning all day.
ד כִּי, יוֹמָם וָלַיְלָה-- תִּכְבַּד עָלַי, יָדֶךָ:	4. For day and night, fear of You lay heavy upon me, my life force dried out as in the scorching summer, *Selah*.
נֶהְפַּךְ לְשַׁדִּי-- בְּחַרְבֹנֵי קַיִץ סֶלָה. ה חַטָּאתִי אוֹדִיעֲךָ, וַעֲוֹנִי לֹא-כִסִּיתִי--	5. I informed You of my sin, and I did not cover my wrongdoing, I said, "I will admit my misdeeds to G-d," and You forgave the wrongdoing of my sin, *Selah*.
אָמַרְתִּי, אוֹדֶה עֲלֵי פְשָׁעַי לַיהוָה; וְאַתָּה נָשָׂאתָ עֲוֹן חַטָּאתִי סֶלָה.	
ו עַל-זֹאת, יִתְפַּלֵּל כָּל-חָסִיד אֵלֶיךָ-- לְעֵת מְצֹא: רַק, לְשֵׁטֶף מַיִם רַבִּים-- אֵלָיו, לֹא יַגִּיעוּ.	6. Therefore, every pious one should pray to you, at a favorable time, so that the raging mighty waters will not overtake him.
ז אַתָּה, סֵתֶר לִי-- מִצַּר תִּצְּרֵנִי: רָנֵּי פַלֵּט; תְּסוֹבְבֵנִי סֶלָה.	7. You are my protection, You guard me against pain, with joyous shouts of deliverance you surround me, *Selah*.

ח אַשְׂכִּילְךָ, וְאוֹרְךָ--בְּדֶרֶךְ-זוּ
תֵלֵךְ; אִיעֲצָה עָלֶיךָ עֵינִי.

8. Let me enlighten you and clarify for you which way to go, my eyes will hint to you.

ט אַל-תִּהְיוּ, כְּסוּס כְּפֶרֶד-- אֵין
הָבִין:
בְּמֶתֶג-וָרֶסֶן עֶדְיוֹ לִבְלוֹם; בַּל,
קְרֹב אֵלֶיךָ.

9. Do not be like a clueless horse or mule, constrained by a mouthpiece and rein while being groomed, so it does not draw near to you.

י רַבִּים מַכְאוֹבִים,
לָרָשָׁע וְהַבּוֹטֵחַ בַּיהוָה--חֶסֶד,
יְסוֹבְבֶנּוּ.

10. Much anguish befalls the wicked, but one who trusts in G-d will be surrounded by kindness.

יא שִׂמְחוּ בַיהוָה וְגִילוּ,
צַדִּיקִים; וְהַרְנִינוּ, כָּל-יִשְׁרֵי-לֵב.

11. Rejoice in G-d, and exult righteous ones, and let all the scrupulous shout for joy.

Psalms Chapter 41

א לַמְנַצֵּחַ, מִזְמוֹר לְדָוִד.

1. A psalm of *Dovid*, to the leading musician.

ב אַשְׁרֵי, מַשְׂכִּיל אֶל-
דָּל; בְּיוֹם רָעָה, יְמַלְּטֵהוּ יְהוָה.

2. Fortunate is the one who is considerate to the disadvantaged, on the day of retribution G-d will save him.

ג יְהוָה, יִשְׁמְרֵהוּ וִיחַיֵּהוּ--יֻאשַּׁר
(וְאֻשַּׁר) בָּאָרֶץ; וְאַל-תִּתְּנֵהוּ,
בְּנֶפֶשׁ אֹיְבָיו.

3. G-d will guard him and give him life, he will be considered happy in the land, and You will not give him over to the will of his enemies

ד יְהוָה--יִסְעָדֶנּוּ, עַל-עֶרֶשׂ
דְּוָי; כָּל-מִשְׁכָּבוֹ, הָפַכְתָּ
בְחָלְיוֹ.

4. G-d will provide for him on his sickbed, You will transform his illness when he is sick.

ה אֲנִי-אָמַרְתִּי, יְהוָה
חָנֵּנִי; רְפָאָה נַפְשִׁי, כִּי-חָטָאתִי
לָךְ.

5. I said, "Let G-d be gracious to me, heal my soul for I have sinned against you."

ו אוֹיְבַי--יֹאמְרוּ רַע לִי; מָתַי
יָמוּת, וְאָבַד שְׁמוֹ.

ז וְאִם-בָּא לִרְאוֹת, שָׁוְא יְדַבֵּר--
לִבּוֹ, יִקְבָּץ-אָוֶן לוֹ; יֵצֵא לַחוּץ
יְדַבֵּר.

ח יַחַד--עָלַי יִתְלַחֲשׁוּ, כָּל-
שֹׂנְאָי; עָלַי--יַחְשְׁבוּ רָעָה לִי.

ט דְּבַר-בְּלִיַּעַל, יָצוּק
בּוֹ; וַאֲשֶׁר שָׁכַב, לֹא-יוֹסִיף
לָקוּם.

י גַּם-אִישׁ שְׁלוֹמִי, אֲשֶׁר-בָּטַחְתִּי
בוֹ-- אוֹכֵל לַחְמִי;
הִגְדִּיל עָלַי עָקֵב.

יא וְאַתָּה יְהוָה, חָנֵּנִי
וַהֲקִימֵנִי; וַאֲשַׁלְּמָה לָהֶם.

יב בְּזֹאת יָדַעְתִּי, כִּי-חָפַצְתָּ
בִּי: כִּי לֹא-יָרִיעַ אֹיְבִי עָלָי.

יג וַאֲנִי--בְּתֻמִּי, תָּמַכְתָּ
בִּי; וַתַּצִּיבֵנִי לְפָנֶיךָ לְעוֹלָם.

יד בָּרוּךְ יְהוָה, אֱלֹהֵי יִשְׂרָאֵל--
מֵהָעוֹלָם, וְעַד הָעוֹלָם: אָמֵן
וְאָמֵן.

6. My enemies speak badly about me, "When will he die, and his name cease."

7. If one comes to visit he speaks dishonestly, his heart accrues evil thoughts, when he leaves he speaks of them.

8. All my antagonist conspire together against me, they plan the worst for me.

9. They say, "His transgression brought about his grief, and now that he is bedridden he will no longer rise."

10. Even my friend whom I trusted, who at my bread, lifted his heel to harm me.

11. But You, G-d be gracious to me and raise me up, and I will pay them their due.

12. Through this, I will know that You yearned for me when my enemies will not shout victoriously over me.

13. Due to my innocence, You will support me, and set me before You forever.

14. Blessed is G-d, G-d of *Yisroel*, from one end of the world to the other, *Amen and Amen.*

Psalms Chapter 42

א לַמְנַצֵּחַ, מַשְׂכִּיל לִבְנֵי-קֹרַח.

1 For the Leader; Maschil of the sons of Korah.

כְּאַיָּל, תַּעֲרֹג עַל-אֲפִיקֵי-מָיִם-- כֵּן **ב**
נַפְשִׁי תַעֲרֹג אֵלֶיךָ אֱלֹהִים.

2 As the hart panteth after the water brooks, so panteth my soul after Thee, O' G-d.

צָמְאָה נַפְשִׁי, לֵאלֹהִים-- לְאֵל חָי **ג**
מָתַי אָבוֹא; וְאֵרָאֶה, פְּנֵי אֱלֹהִים.

3 My soul thirsts for G-d, for the living G-d: 'When shall I come and appear before G-d?'

הָיְתָה-לִּי דִמְעָתִי לֶחֶם, יוֹמָם **ד**
וָלָיְלָה;
בֶּאֱמֹר אֵלַי כָּל-הַיּוֹם, אַיֵּה אֱלֹהֶיךָ.

4 My tears have been my food day and night, while they say unto me all the day: 'Where is thy G-d?'

אֵלֶּה אֶזְכְּרָה, וְאֶשְׁפְּכָה עָלַי נַפְשִׁי **ה**
--
כִּי אֶעֱבֹר בַּסָּךְ, אֶדַּדֵּם עַד-בֵּית
אֱלֹהִים:
הֲמוֹן חוֹגֵג בְּקוֹל-רִנָּה וְתוֹדָה;

5 These things I remember and pour out my soul within me, how I passed on with the throng, and led them to the house of G-d, with the voice of joy and praise, a multitude keeping holyday.

מַה-תִּשְׁתּוֹחֲחִי, נַפְשִׁי-- וַתֶּהֱמִי **ו**
עָלָי:
הוֹחִלִי לֵאלֹהִים, כִּי-עוֹד אוֹדֶנּוּ--
יְשׁוּעוֹת פָּנָיו.

6 Why art thou cast down, O' my soul? and why moanest thou within me? Hope thou in G-d; for I shall yet praise Him for the salvation of His countenance.

אֱלֹהַי-- עָלַי, נַפְשִׁי תִשְׁתּוֹחָח **ז**
עַל-כֵּן--אֶזְכָּרְךָ, מֵאֶרֶץ
יַרְדֵּן; וְחֶרְמוֹנִים, מֵהַר מִצְעָר.

7 O my G-d, my soul is cast down within me; therefore, do I remember Thee from the land of Jordan, and the Hermons, from the hill Mizar.

תְּהוֹם-אֶל-תְּהוֹם קוֹרֵא, לְקוֹל **ח**
צִנּוֹרֶיךָ;
כָּל-מִשְׁבָּרֶיךָ וְגַלֶּיךָ, עָלַי עָבָרוּ.

8 Deep calleth unto deep at the voice of Thy cataracts; all Thy waves and Thy billows are gone over me.

יוֹמָם, יְצַוֶּה יְהוָה **ט**
חַסְדּוֹ, וּבַלַּיְלָה, שִׁירֹה עִמִּי--
תְּפִלָּה, לְאֵל חַיָּי.

9 By day the L-RD will command His loving-kindness, and in the night His song shall be with me, even a prayer unto the G-d of my life.

אוֹמְרָה, לְאֵל סַלְעִי-- לָמָה **י**
שְׁכַחְתָּנִי:
לָמָּה-קֹדֵר אֵלֵךְ-- בְּלַחַץ אוֹיֵב.

10 I will say unto G-d my Rock: 'Why hast Thou has forgotten me? Why go I mourning under the oppression of the enemy?'

123

חֵרְפוּנִי **יא** צוֹרְרָי; בְּרֶצַח, בְּעַצְמוֹתַי-- בְּאָמְרָם אֵלַי כָּל-הַיּוֹם, אַיֵּה אֱלֹהֶיךָ.	**11** As with a crushing in my bones, mine adversaries taunt me; while they say unto me all the day: 'Where is thy G-d?'
וּמַה- **יב** מַה-תִּשְׁתּוֹחֲחִי, נַפְשִׁי-- עָלָי תֶּהֱמִי: הוֹחִילִי לֵאלֹהִים, כִּי-עוֹד אוֹדֶנּוּ-- יְשׁוּעֹת פָּנַי, וֵאלֹהָי -.	**12** Why art thou cast down, O my soul? and why moanest thou within me? Hope thou in G-d; for I shall yet praise Him, the salvation of my countenance, and my G-d.

Psalms Chapter 59

א לַמְנַצֵּחַ אַל-תַּשְׁחֵת, לְדָוִד מִכְתָּם: בִּשְׁלֹחַ שָׁאוּל; וַיִּשְׁמְרוּ אֶת-הַבַּיִת, לַהֲמִיתוֹ.	**1** For the Leader; Al-*tashheth*. [A Psalm] of David; Michtam; when Saul sent, and they watched the house to kill him.
ב הַצִּילֵנִי מֵאֹיְבַי אֱלֹהָי; מִמִּתְקוֹמְמַי תְּשַׂגְּבֵנִי.	**2** Deliver me from mine enemies, O my G-d; set me on high from them that rise up against me.
ג הַצִּילֵנִי, מִפֹּעֲלֵי אָוֶן; וּמֵאַנְשֵׁי דָמִים, הוֹשִׁיעֵנִי.	**3** Deliver me from the workers of iniquity, and save me from the men of blood.
ד כִּי הִנֵּה אָרְבוּ, לְנַפְשִׁי-- יָגוּרוּ עָלַי עַזִּים; לֹא-פִשְׁעִי וְלֹא-חַטָּאתִי יְהוָה.	**4** For, lo, they lie in wait for my soul; the impudent gather themselves together against me; not for my transgression, nor for my sin, O' L-RD.
ה בְּלִי-עָוֹן, יְרֻצוּן וְיִכּוֹנָנוּ; עוּרָה לִקְרָאתִי וּרְאֵה.	**5** Without my fault, they run and prepare themselves; awake Thou to help me and behold.
ו וְאַתָּה יְהוָה-אֱלֹהִים צְבָאוֹת, אֱלֹהֵי יִשְׂרָאֵל-- הָקִיצָה, לִפְקֹד כָּל-הַגּוֹיִם; אַל-תָּחֹן כָּל-בֹּגְדֵי אָוֶן סֶלָה.	**6** Thou, therefore, O' L-RD G-d of hosts, the G-d of Israel, arouse Thyself to punish all the nations; show no mercy to any iniquitous traitors. Selah

ז יָשׁוּבוּ לָעֶרֶב, יֶהֱמוּ כַכָּלֶב; וִיסוֹבְבוּ עִיר.

7 They return at evening, they howl like a dog and go round about the city.

ח הִנֵּה, יַבִּיעוּן בְּפִיהֶם--חֲרָבוֹת, בְּשִׂפְתוֹתֵיהֶם: כִּי-מִי שֹׁמֵעַ.

8 Behold, they belch out with their mouth; swords are in their lips: 'For who doth hear?'

ט וְאַתָּה יְהוָה, תִּשְׂחַק-לָמוֹ; תִּלְעַג, לְכָל-גּוֹיִם.

9 But Thou, O' L-RD, shalt laugh at them; Thou shalt have all the nations in derision.

י עֻזּוֹ, אֵלֶיךָ אֶשְׁמֹרָה: כִּי-אֱלֹהִים, מִשְׂגַּבִּי.

10 Because of his strength, I will wait for Thee; for G-d is my high tower.

יא אֱלֹהֵי חסדו (חַסְדִּי) יְקַדְּמֵנִי; אֱלֹהִים, יַרְאֵנִי בְשֹׁרְרָי.

11 The G-d of my mercy will come to meet me; G-d will let me gaze upon mine adversaries.

יב אַל-תַּהַרְגֵם, פֶּן יִשְׁכְּחוּ עַמִּי--הֲנִיעֵמוֹ בְחֵילְךָ, וְהוֹרִידֵמוֹ: מָגִנֵּנוּ אֲדֹנָי.

12 Slay them not, lest my people forget, make them wander to and fro by Thy power, and bring them down, O' L-rd our shield.

יג חַטַּאת-פִּימוֹ, דְּבַר-שְׂפָתֵימוֹ; וְיִלָּכְדוּ בִגְאוֹנָם; וּמֵאָלָה וּמִכַּחַשׁ יְסַפֵּרוּ.

13 For the sin of their mouth, and the words of their lips, let them even be taken in their pride, and for cursing and lying which they speak.

יד כַּלֵּה בְחֵמָה, כַּלֵּה וְאֵינֵמוֹ: וְיֵדְעוּ--כִּי-אֱלֹהִים, מֹשֵׁל בְּיַעֲקֹב; לְאַפְסֵי הָאָרֶץ סֶלָה.

14 Consume them in wrath, consume them, that they be no more; and let them know that G-d ruleth in Jacob, unto the ends of the earth. Selah

טו וְיָשֻׁבוּ לָעֶרֶב, יֶהֱמוּ כַכָּלֶב; וִיסוֹבְבוּ עִיר.

15 And they return at evening, they howl like a dog, and go round about the city;

טז הֵמָּה, ינועון (יְנִיעוּן) לֶאֱכֹל-- אִם-לֹא יִשְׂבְּעוּ, וַיָּלִינוּ.

16 They wander up and down to devour and tarry all night if they have not their fill.

125

| יז וַאֲנִי, אָשִׁיר עֻזֶּךָ-- וַאֲרַנֵּן לַבֹּקֶר, חַסְדֶּךָ: כִּי-הָיִיתָ מִשְׂגָּב לִי; וּמָנוֹס, בְּיוֹם צַר-לִי. | 17 But as for me, I will sing of Thy strength; yea, I will sing aloud of Thy mercy in the morning; for Thou hast been my high tower, and a refuge in the day of my distress. |
| יח עֻזִּי, אֵלֶיךָ אֲזַמֵּרָה: כִּי-אֱלֹהִים מִשְׂגַּבִּי, אֱלֹהֵי חַסְדִּי. | 18 O' my strength, unto Thee will I sing praises; for G-d is my high tower, the G-d of my mercy. |

Psalms Chapter 77

א לַמְנַצֵּחַ עַל-יְדִיתוּן (יְדוּתוּן); לְאָסָף מִזְמוֹר.	1 For the Leader; for Jeduthun. A Psalm of Asaph.
ב קוֹלִי אֶל-אֱלֹהִים וְאֶצְעָקָה; קוֹלִי אֶל-אֱלֹהִים, וְהַאֲזִין אֵלָי.	2 I will lift up my voice unto G-d, and cry; I will lift up my voice unto G-d, that He may give ear unto me.
ג בְּיוֹם צָרָתִי, אֲדֹנָי דָּרָשְׁתִּי: יָדִי, לַיְלָה נִגְּרָה--וְלֹא תָפוּג; מֵאֲנָה הִנָּחֵם נַפְשִׁי.	3 In the day of my trouble I seek the L-rd; with my hand uplifted, [mine eye] streameth in the night without ceasing; my soul refuseth to be comforted.
ד אֶזְכְּרָה אֱלֹהִים וְאֶהֱמָיָה; אָשִׂיחָה, וְתִתְעַטֵּף רוּחִי סֶלָה.	4 When I think thereon, O' G-d, I must moan; when I muse thereon, my spirit fainteth. Selah
ה אָחַזְתָּ, שְׁמֻרוֹת עֵינָי; נִפְעַמְתִּי, וְלֹא אֲדַבֵּר.	5 Thou holdest fast the lids of mine eyes; I am troubled, and cannot speak.
ו חִשַּׁבְתִּי יָמִים מִקֶּדֶם-- שְׁנוֹת, עוֹלָמִים.	6 I have pondered the days of old, the years of ancient times.
ז אֶזְכְּרָה נְגִינָתִי, בַּלָּיְלָה: עִם-לְבָבִי אָשִׂיחָה; וַיְחַפֵּשׂ רוּחִי.	7 In the night I will call to remembrance my song; I will commune with mine own heart; and my spirit maketh diligent search:

ח הַלְעוֹלָמִים, יִזְנַח אֲדֹנָי; וְלֹא-יֹסִיף לִרְצוֹת עוֹד.	8 'Will the L-rd cast off forever? And will He be favorable no more?
ט הֶאָפֵס לָנֶצַח חַסְדּוֹ; גָּמַר אֹמֶר, לְדֹר וָדֹר.	9 Is His mercy clean gone forever? Is His promise come to an end for evermore?
י הֲשָׁכַח חַנּוֹת אֵל; אִם-קָפַץ בְּאַף, רַחֲמָיו סֶלָה.	10 Hath G-d forgotten to be gracious? Hath He in anger shut up his compassions?' Selah
יא וָאֹמַר, חַלּוֹתִי הִיא-- שְׁנוֹת, יְמִין עֶלְיוֹן.	11 And I say: 'This is my weakness, that the right hand of the Most High could change.
יב אזכיר (אֶזְכּוֹר) מַעַלְלֵי-יָהּ: כִּי-אֶזְכְּרָה מִקֶּדֶם פִּלְאֶךָ.	12 I will make mention of the deeds of the L-RD; yea, I will remember Thy wonders of old.
יג וְהָגִיתִי בְכָל-פָּעֳלֶךָ; וּבַעֲלִילוֹתֶיךָ אָשִׂיחָה.	13 I will meditate also upon all Thy work, and muse on Thy doings.'
יד אֱלֹהִים, בַּקֹּדֶשׁ דַּרְכֶּךָ; מִי-אֵל גָּדוֹל, כֵּאלֹהִים.	14 O' G-d, Thy way is in holiness; who is a great G-d like unto G-d?
טו אַתָּה הָאֵל, עֹשֵׂה פֶלֶא; הוֹדַעְתָּ בָעַמִּים עֻזֶּךָ.	15 Thou art the G-d that doest wonders; Thou hast made known Thy strength among the peoples.
טז גָּאַלְתָּ בִּזְרוֹעַ עַמֶּךָ; בְּנֵי-יַעֲקֹב וְיוֹסֵף סֶלָה.	16 Thou hast with Thine arm redeemed Thy people, the sons of Jacob and Joseph. Selah
יז רָאוּךָ מַּיִם, אֱלֹהִים--רָאוּךָ מַּיִם יָחִילוּ; אַף, יִרְגְּזוּ תְהֹמוֹת.	17 The waters saw Thee, O' G-d; the waters saw Thee, they were in pain; the depths also trembled.
יח זֹרְמוּ מַיִם, עָבוֹת--קוֹל, נָתְנוּ שְׁחָקִים; אַף-חֲצָצֶיךָ, יִתְהַלָּכוּ.	18 The clouds flooded forth waters; the skies sent out a sound; Thine arrows also went abroad.
יט קוֹל רַעַמְךָ, בַּגַּלְגַּל--הֵאִירוּ בְרָקִים תֵּבֵל; רָגְזָה וַתִּרְעַשׁ הָאָרֶץ.	19 The voice of Thy thunder was in the whirlwind; the lightnings lighted

up the world; the earth trembled and
shook.

כ בַּיָּם דַּרְכֶּךָ--וּשְׁבִילְיךָ (וּשְׁבִילְךָ), בְּמַיִם
רַבִּים; וְעִקְּבוֹתֶיךָ, לֹא נֹדָעוּ. **20** Thy way was in the sea, and Thy
path in the great waters, and Thy
footsteps were not known.

כא נָחִיתָ כַצֹּאן עַמֶּךָ-- בְּיַד-מֹשֶׁה וְאַהֲרֹן. **21** Thou didst lead Thy people like a
flock, by the hand of Moses and
Aaron.

Psalms Chapter 90

א תְּפִלָּה, לְמֹשֶׁה אִישׁ-הָאֱלֹהִים:
אֲדֹנָי--מָעוֹן אַתָּה, הָיִיתָ לָּנוּ; בְּדֹר וָדֹר. **1** A Prayer of Moses the man of G-d.
L-rd, Thou hast been our dwelling-
place in all generations.

ב בְּטֶרֶם, הָרִים יֻלָּדוּ-- וַתְּחוֹלֵל אֶרֶץ
וְתֵבֵל;
וּמֵעוֹלָם עַד-עוֹלָם, אַתָּה אֵל. **2** Before the mountains were brought
forth, or ever Thou hadst formed the
earth and the world, even from
everlasting to everlasting, Thou art
G-d.

ג תָּשֵׁב אֱנוֹשׁ, עַד-דַּכָּא; וַתֹּאמֶר, שׁוּבוּ
בְנֵי-אָדָם. **3** Thou turnest man to contrition; and
sayest: 'Return, ye children of men.'

ד כִּי אֶלֶף שָׁנִים, בְּעֵינֶיךָ-- כְּיוֹם אֶתְמוֹל,
כִּי יַעֲבֹר;
וְאַשְׁמוּרָה בַלָּיְלָה. **4** For a thousand years in Thy sight
are but as yesterday when it is past,
and as a watch in the night.

ה זְרַמְתָּם, שֵׁנָה יִהְיוּ; בַּבֹּקֶר, כֶּחָצִיר
יַחֲלֹף. **5** Thou carriest them away as with a
flood; they are as a sleep; in the
morning they are like grass which
groweth up.

ו בַּבֹּקֶר, יָצִיץ וְחָלָף; לָעֶרֶב, יְמוֹלֵל וְיָבֵשׁ. **6** In the morning it flourisheth, and
groweth up; in the evening it is cut
down, and withereth.

ז כִּי-כָלִינוּ בְאַפֶּךָ; וּבַחֲמָתְךָ נִבְהָלְנוּ

7 For we are consumed in Thine anger, and by Thy wrath are we hurried away.

ח שת (שַׁתָּה) עֲוֺנֹתֵינוּ לְנֶגְדֶּךָ; עֲלֻמֵנוּ, לִמְאוֹר פָּנֶיךָ.

8 Thou hast set our iniquities before Thee, our secret sins in the light of Thy countenance.

ט כִּי כָל-יָמֵינוּ, פָּנוּ בְעֶבְרָתֶךָ; כִּלִּינוּ שָׁנֵינוּ כְמוֹ-הֶגֶה.

9 For all our days are passed away in Thy wrath; we bring our years to an end as a tale that is told.

י יְמֵי-שְׁנוֹתֵינוּ בָהֶם שִׁבְעִים שָׁנָה, וְאִם בִּגְבוּרֹת שְׁמוֹנִים שָׁנָה— וְרָהְבָּם, עָמָל וָאָוֶן: כִּי-גָז חִישׁ, וַנָּעֻפָה.

10 The days of our years are threescore years and ten, or even by reason of strength fourscore years; yet is their pride but travail and vanity; for it is speedily gone, and we fly away.

יא מִי-יוֹדֵעַ, עֹז אַפֶּךָ; וּכְיִרְאָתְךָ, עֶבְרָתֶךָ.

11 Who knoweth the power of Thine anger, and Thy wrath according to the fear that is due unto Thee?

יב לִמְנוֹת יָמֵינוּ, כֵּן הוֹדַע; וְנָבָא, לְבַב חָכְמָה.

12 So teach us to number our days, that we may get us a heart of wisdom.

יג שׁוּבָה יְהוָה, עַד-מָתָי; וְהִנָּחֵם, עַל-עֲבָדֶיךָ.

13 Return, O' L-RD; how long? And let it repent Thee concerning Thy servants.

יד שַׂבְּעֵנוּ בַבֹּקֶר חַסְדֶּךָ; וּנְרַנְּנָה וְנִשְׂמְחָה, בְּכָל-יָמֵינוּ.

14 O satisfy us in the morning with Thy mercy; that we may rejoice and be glad all our days.

טו שַׂמְּחֵנוּ, כִּימוֹת עִנִּיתָנוּ: שְׁנוֹת, רָאִינוּ רָעָה.

15 Make us glad according to the days wherein Thou hast afflicted us, according to the years wherein we have seen evil.

טז יֵרָאֶה אֶל-עֲבָדֶיךָ פָעֳלֶךָ; וַהֲדָרְךָ, עַל-בְּנֵיהֶם.

16 Let Thy work appear unto Thy servants and Thy glory upon their children.

יז וִיהִי, נֹעַם אֲדֹנָי אֱלֹהֵינוּ-- עָלֵינוּ: וּמַעֲשֵׂה יָדֵינוּ, כּוֹנְנָה עָלֵינוּ; וּמַעֲשֵׂה יָדֵינוּ, כּוֹנְנֵהוּ.

17 And let the graciousness of the L-rd our G-d be upon us; establish Thou also upon us the work of our hands; yea, the work of our hands establish Thou it.

Psalms Chapter 105

א הוֹדוּ לַיהוָה, קִרְאוּ בִשְׁמוֹ; הוֹדִיעוּ בָעַמִּים, עֲלִילוֹתָיו.

1 O' give thanks unto the L-RD, call upon His name; make known His doings among the peoples.

ב שִׁירוּ-לוֹ, זַמְּרוּ-לוֹ; שִׂיחוּ, בְּכָל-נִפְלְאוֹתָיו.

2 Sing unto Him, sing praises unto Him; speak ye of all His marvelous works.

ג הִתְהַלְלוּ, בְּשֵׁם קָדְשׁוֹ; יִשְׂמַח, לֵב מְבַקְשֵׁי יְהוָה.

3 Glory ye in His holy name; let the heart of them rejoice that seek the L-RD.

ד דִּרְשׁוּ יְהוָה וְעֻזּוֹ; בַּקְּשׁוּ פָנָיו תָּמִיד.

4 Seek ye the L-RD and His strength; seek His face continually.

ה זִכְרוּ--נִפְלְאוֹתָיו אֲשֶׁר-עָשָׂה; מֹפְתָיו, וּמִשְׁפְּטֵי-פִיו.

5 Remember His marvelous works that He hath done, His wonders, and the judgments of His mouth;

ו זֶרַע, אַבְרָהָם עַבְדּוֹ: בְּנֵי יַעֲקֹב בְּחִירָיו.

6 O' ye seed of Abraham His servant, ye children of Jacob, His chosen ones.

ז הוּא, יְהוָה אֱלֹהֵינוּ; בְּכָל-הָאָרֶץ, מִשְׁפָּטָיו.

7 He is the L-RD our G-d; His judgments are in all the earth.

ח זָכַר לְעוֹלָם בְּרִיתוֹ; דָּבָר צִוָּה, לְאֶלֶף דּוֹר.

8 He hath remembered His covenant forever, the word which He commanded to a thousand generations;

ט אֲשֶׁר כָּרַת, אֶת-אַבְרָהָם; וּשְׁבוּעָתוֹ לְיִשְׂחָק.

9 [The covenant] which He made with Abraham, and His oath unto Isaac;

10 And He established it unto Jacob for a statute, to Israel for an everlasting covenant;

י וַיַּעֲמִידֶהָ לְיַעֲקֹב לְחֹק; לְיִשְׂרָאֵל, בְּרִית עוֹלָם.

11 Saying: 'Unto thee will I give the Land of Canaan, the lot of your inheritance.'

יא לֵאמֹר--לְךָ, אֶתֵּן אֶת-אֶרֶץ-כְּנָעַן: חֶבֶל, נַחֲלַתְכֶם.

12 When they were but a few men in number. Yea, very few, and sojourners in it,

יב בִּהְיוֹתָם, מְתֵי מִסְפָּר; כִּמְעַט, וְגָרִים בָּהּ.

13 And when they went about from nation to nation, from one kingdom to another people,

יג וַיִּתְהַלְּכוּ, מִגּוֹי אֶל-גּוֹי; מִמַּמְלָכָה, אֶל-עַם אַחֵר.

14 He suffered no man to do them wrong, yea, for their sake He reproved kings:

יד לֹא-הִנִּיחַ אָדָם לְעָשְׁקָם; וַיּוֹכַח עֲלֵיהֶם מְלָכִים.

15 'Touch not Mine anointed ones, and do My prophets no harm.'

טו אַל-תִּגְּעוּ בִמְשִׁיחָי; וְלִנְבִיאַי, אַל-תָּרֵעוּ.

16 And He called a famine upon the land; He broke the whole staff of bread.

טז וַיִּקְרָא רָעָב, עַל-הָאָרֶץ; כָּל-מַטֵּה-לֶחֶם שָׁבָר.

17 He sent a man before them; Joseph was sold for a servant;

יז שָׁלַח לִפְנֵיהֶם אִישׁ; לְעֶבֶד, נִמְכַּר יוֹסֵף.

18 His feet they hurt with fetters, his person was laid in iron;

יח עִנּוּ בַכֶּבֶל רגליו (רַגְלוֹ); בַּרְזֶל, בָּאָה נַפְשׁוֹ.

19 Until the time that his word came to pass, the word of the L-RD tested him.

יט עַד-עֵת בֹּא-דְבָרוֹ-- אִמְרַת יְהוָה צְרָפָתְהוּ.

20 The king sent and loosed him; even the ruler of the peoples, and set him free.

כ שָׁלַח מֶלֶךְ, וַיַּתִּירֵהוּ; מֹשֵׁל עַמִּים, וַיְפַתְּחֵהוּ.

21 He made him L-RD of his house, and ruler of all his possessions;

כא שָׂמוֹ אָדוֹן לְבֵיתוֹ; וּמֹשֵׁל, בְּכָל-קִנְיָנוֹ.

כב לֶאְסֹר שָׂרָיו בְּנַפְשׁוֹ; וּזְקֵנָיו יְחַכֵּם.

22 To bind his princes at his pleasure, and teach his elders wisdom.

כג וַיָּבֹא יִשְׂרָאֵל מִצְרָיִם; וְיַעֲקֹב, גָּר בְּאֶרֶץ-חָם.

23 Israel also came into Egypt; and Jacob sojourned in the Land of Ham.

כד וַיֶּפֶר אֶת-עַמּוֹ מְאֹד; וַיַּעֲצִמֵהוּ, מִצָּרָיו.

24 And He increased His people greatly, and made them too mighty for their adversaries.

כה הָפַךְ לִבָּם, לִשְׂנֹא עַמּוֹ; לְהִתְנַכֵּל, בַּעֲבָדָיו.

25 He turned their heart to hate His people, to deal craftily with His servants.

כו שָׁלַח, מֹשֶׁה עַבְדּוֹ; אַהֲרֹן, אֲשֶׁר בָּחַר-בּוֹ.

26 He sent Moses His servant, and Aaron whom He had chosen.

כז שָׂמוּ-בָם, דִּבְרֵי אֹתוֹתָיו; וּמֹפְתִים, בְּאֶרֶץ חָם.

27 They wrought among them His manifold signs, and wonders in the Land of Ham.

כח שָׁלַח חֹשֶׁךְ, וַיַּחְשִׁךְ; וְלֹא-מָרוּ, אֶת-דבריו (דְּבָרוֹ).

28 He sent darkness, and it was dark; and they rebelled not against His word.

כט הָפַךְ אֶת-מֵימֵיהֶם לְדָם; וַיָּמֶת, אֶת-דְּגָתָם.

29 He turned their waters into blood, and slew their fish.

ל שָׁרַץ אַרְצָם צְפַרְדְּעִים; בְּחַדְרֵי, מַלְכֵיהֶם.

30 Their land swarmed with frogs, in the chambers of their kings.

לא אָמַר, וַיָּבֹא עָרֹב; כִּנִּים, בְּכָל-גְּבוּלָם.

31 He spoke, and there came swarms of flies, and gnats in all their borders.

לב נָתַן גִּשְׁמֵיהֶם בָּרָד; אֵשׁ לֶהָבוֹת בְּאַרְצָם.

32 He gave them hail for rain, and flaming fire in their land.

לג וַיַּךְ גַּפְנָם, וּתְאֵנָתָם; וַיְשַׁבֵּר, עֵץ גְּבוּלָם.

33 He smote their vines also and their fig trees; and broke the trees of their borders.

לד אָמַר, וַיָּבֹא אַרְבֶּה; וְיֶלֶק, וְאֵין מִסְפָּר.	34 He spoke, and the locust came, and the canker-worm without number,
לה וַיֹּאכַל כָּל-עֵשֶׂב בְּאַרְצָם; וַיֹּאכַל, פְּרִי אַדְמָתָם.	35 And did eat up every herb in their land, and did eat up the fruit of their ground.
לו וַיַּךְ כָּל-בְּכוֹר בְּאַרְצָם; רֵאשִׁית, לְכָל-אוֹנָם.	36 He smote also all the first-born in their land, the first-fruits of all their strength.
לז וַיּוֹצִיאֵם, בְּכֶסֶף וְזָהָב; וְאֵין בִּשְׁבָטָיו כּוֹשֵׁל.	37 And He brought them forth with silver and gold; and there was none that stumbled among His tribes.
לח שָׂמַח מִצְרַיִם בְּצֵאתָם: כִּי-נָפַל פַּחְדָּם עֲלֵיהֶם.	38 Egypt was glad when they departed; for the fear of them had fallen upon them.
לט פָּרַשׂ עָנָן לְמָסָךְ; וְאֵשׁ, לְהָאִיר לָיְלָה.	39 He spread a cloud for a screen; and fire to give light in the night.
מ שָׁאַל, וַיָּבֵא שְׂלָו; וְלֶחֶם שָׁמַיִם, יַשְׂבִּיעֵם.	40 They asked, and He brought quails, and gave them in plenty the bread of heaven.
מא פָּתַח צוּר, וַיָּזוּבוּ מָיִם; הָלְכוּ, בַּצִּיּוֹת נָהָר.	41 He opened the rock, and waters gushed out; they ran, a river in the dry places.
מב כִּי-זָכַר, אֶת-דְּבַר קָדְשׁוֹ; אֶת-אַבְרָהָם עַבְדּוֹ.	42 For He remembered His holy word unto Abraham His servant;
מג וַיּוֹצִא עַמּוֹ בְשָׂשׂוֹן; בְּרִנָּה, אֶת-בְּחִירָיו.	43 And He brought forth His people with joy, His chosen ones with singing.
מד וַיִּתֵּן לָהֶם, אַרְצוֹת גּוֹיִם; וַעֲמַל לְאֻמִּים יִירָשׁוּ.	44 And He gave them the lands of the nations, and they took the labor of the peoples in possession;

מַה בַּעֲבוּר, יִשְׁמְרוּ חֻקָּיו-- וְתוֹרֹתָיו יִנְצֹרוּ; הַלְלוּ-יָהּ.	**45** That they might keep His statutes, and observe His laws. Halleluyah.

Psalms Chapter 137

א עַל נַהֲרוֹת, בָּבֶל--שָׁם יָשַׁבְנוּ, גַּם-בָּכִינוּ: בְּזָכְרֵנוּ, אֶת-צִיּוֹן.	**1** By the rivers of Babylon, there we sat down, yea, we wept, when we remembered Zion.
ב עַל-עֲרָבִים בְּתוֹכָהּ-- תָּלִינוּ, כִּנֹּרוֹתֵינוּ.	**2** Upon the willows in the midst thereof we hanged up our harps.
ג כִּי שָׁם שְׁאֵלוּנוּ שׁוֹבֵינוּ, דִּבְרֵי-שִׁיר-- וְתוֹלָלֵינוּ שִׂמְחָה: שִׁירוּ לָנוּ, מִשִּׁיר צִיּוֹן.	**3** For there they that led us captive asked of us words of song, and our tormentors asked of us mirth: 'Sing us one of the songs of Zion.'
ד אֵיךְ--נָשִׁיר אֶת-שִׁיר-יְהוָה: עַל, אַדְמַת נֵכָר.	**4** How shall we sing the L-RD'S song in a foreign land?
ה אִם-אֶשְׁכָּחֵךְ יְרוּשָׁלִָם-- תִּשְׁכַּח יְמִינִי.	**5** If I forget thee, O' Jerusalem, let my right hand forget her cunning.
ו תִּדְבַּק-לְשׁוֹנִי, לְחִכִּי-- אִם-לֹא אֶזְכְּרֵכִי: אִם-לֹא אַעֲלֶה, אֶת-יְרוּשָׁלִַם-- עַל, רֹאשׁ שִׂמְחָתִי.	**6** Let my tongue cleave to the roof of my mouth, if I remember thee not; if I set not Jerusalem above my chiefest joy.
ז זְכֹר יְהוָה, לִבְנֵי אֱדוֹם-- אֵת, יוֹם יְרוּשָׁלִָם: הָאֹמְרִים, עָרוּ עָרוּ-- עַד, הַיְסוֹד בָּהּ.	**7** Remember, O' L-RD, against the children of Edom the day of Jerusalem; who said: 'Raze it, raze it, even to the foundation thereof.'
ח בַּת-בָּבֶל, הַשְּׁדוּדָה: אַשְׁרֵי שֶׁיְשַׁלֶּם-לָךְ-- אֶת-גְּמוּלֵךְ, שֶׁגָּמַלְתְּ לָנוּ.	**8** O' daughter of Babylon, that art to be destroyed; happy shall he be, that repayeth thee as thou hast served us.
ט אַשְׁרֵי, שֶׁיֹּאחֵז וְנִפֵּץ אֶת-עֹלָלַיִךְ-- אֶל-הַסָּלַע.	**9** Happy shall he be, that taketh and dasheth thy little ones against the rock.

Psalms Chapter 150

א הַלְלוּ-יָהּ: הַלְלוּ-אֵל בְּקָדְשׁוֹ; הַלְלוּהוּ, בִּרְקִיעַ עֻזּוֹ.	1 Halleluyah. Praise G-d in His sanctuary; praise Him in the firmament of His power.
ב הַלְלוּהוּ בִגְבוּרֹתָיו; הַלְלוּהוּ, כְּרֹב גֻּדְלוֹ.	2 Praise Him for His mighty acts; praise Him according to His abundant greatness.
ג הַלְלוּהוּ, בְּתֵקַע שׁוֹפָר; הַלְלוּהוּ, בְּנֵבֶל וְכִנּוֹר.	3 Praise Him with the blast of the horn; praise Him with the psaltery and harp.
ד הַלְלוּהוּ, בְּתֹף וּמָחוֹל; הַלְלוּהוּ, בְּמִנִּים וְעֻגָב.	4 Praise Him with the timbrel and dance; praise Him with stringed instruments and the pipe.
ה הַלְלוּהוּ בְצִלְצְלֵי-שָׁמַע; הַלְלוּהוּ, בְּצִלְצְלֵי תְרוּעָה.	5 Praise Him with the loud-sounding cymbals; praise Him with the clanging cymbals.
ו כֹּל הַנְּשָׁמָה, תְּהַלֵּל יָהּ: הַלְלוּ-יָהּ.	6 Let everything that hath breath praise the L-RD. Halleluyah.

Perek Shirah

וְאוּלָם שְׁאַל־נָא בְהֵמוֹת וְתֹרֶךָּ	But ask now the animals, and they shall teach you;
וְעוֹף הַשָּׁמַיִם וְיַגֶּד־לָךְ:	And the birds of the sky, and they shall tell you;
אוֹ שִׂיחַ לָאָרֶץ וְתֹרֶךָּ	Or speak to the Earth, and it shall teach you;
וִיסַפְּרוּ לְךָ דְּגֵי הַיָּם:	And the fishes of the sea shall declare unto you;
מִי לֹא־יָדַע בְּכָל־אֵלֶּה כִּי יַד־ יְהוָה עָשְׂתָה זֹּאת:	Who knows not among all these, That the hand of HaShem has wrought this?
אֲשֶׁר בְּיָדוֹ נֶפֶשׁ כָּל־חָי וְרוּחַ כָּל־בְּשַׂר־אִישׁ:	In whose hand is the soul of every living thing, And the breath of all humanity.

הַקְדָּמָה	**Introductory Text**
אָמַר רַבִּי אֱלִיעֶזֶר, כָּל הָעוֹסֵק בְּפֶרֶק שִׁירָה בָּעוֹלָם הַזֶּה זוֹכֶה וְאוֹמְרָהּ לְעוֹלָם הַבָּא שֶׁנֶּאֱמַר "אָז יָשִׁיר מֹשֶׁה" – "שָׁר" לֹא נֶאֱמַר אֶלָּא "יָשִׁיר" לְעוֹלָם הַבָּא:	Rabbi Eliezer said: Anyone who involves himself with Perek Shirah in this world, merits saying it in the World-to-Come, as it says, "Then Moshe will sing"; it does not say "sang," but "will sing" in the World-to-Come.
וְאָמַר רַבִּי כָּל הָעוֹסֵק בְּפֶרֶק שִׁירָה בָּעוֹלָם הַזֶּה מֵעִיד אֲנִי עָלָיו שֶׁהוּא בֶּן עוֹלָם הַבָּא וְנִצּוֹל מִיֵּצֶר הָרָע וּמִדִּין קָשֶׁה וּמִשָּׂטָן הַמַּשְׁחִית וּמִכָּל מִינֵי מַזִּיקִין וּמֵחֶבְלוֹ שֶׁל מָשִׁיחַ וּמִדִּינָהּ שֶׁל גֵּיהִנֹּם וְזוֹכֶה לִלְמוֹד וּלְלַמֵּד לִשְׁמוֹר וְלַעֲשׂוֹת וּלְקַיֵּים וְתַלְמוּדוֹ מִקְיֵּים בְּיָדוֹ וּמַאֲרִיךְ יָמִים וְזוֹכֶה לְחַיֵּי עוֹלָם הַבָּא:	And Rebbi said: Anyone who involves himself with Perek Shirah in this world - I testify that he is destined for the World-to-Come, and he is saved from the evil inclination, and from harsh judgment, and from the destroying Satan, and from all types of enemies, and from the birth pangs of Mashiah, and from the judgment of Gehinnom; and he merits to learn and to teach, to observe and to fulfill and to perform [the Torah], and his studies are established in him, and his days are lengthened, and he merits life in the World-to-Come.

[Yalkut Shimoni, end of Psalms]The Sages said concerning King David that when he completed the book of Psalms, he became proud. He said before the Holy One, Blessed be He, "Is there any creature You have created in Your world that says more songs and praises than I?" At that moment a frog happened across his path, and it said to him: David! Do not become proud, for I recite more songs and praises than you. Furthermore, every song I say contains three thousand parables, as it says, "And he spoke three thousand parables, and his songs were one thousand five hundred." And furthermore, I am busy with a great mitzvah, and this is the mitzvah with which I am busy – there is a certain type of creature by the edge of the sea whose sustenance is entirely from [creatures living in] the water, and when it is hungry, it takes me and eats me, such that I fulfill that which it says, "If your enemy is hungry, feed him; if he is thirsty, give him water to drink; for you shall heap coals of fire on his head, and G-d shall reward you"; do not read "shall reward you" but instead "shall make him complete you."

(יַלְקוּט, סוֹף תְּהִלִּים) אָמְרוּ רַבּוֹתֵינוּ ז"ל עַל דָּוִד הַמֶּלֶךְ ע"ה בְּשָׁעָה שֶׁסִּיֵּם סֵפֶר תְּהִלִּים זָחָה דַעְתּוֹ עָלָיו. אָמַר לִפְנֵי הַקָּדוֹשׁ בָּרוּךְ הוּא "יֵשׁ בְּרִיאָה שֶׁבָּרֵאתָ בְּעוֹלָמְךְ שֶׁאוֹמֶרֶת שִׁירוֹת וְתִשְׁבָּחוֹת יוֹתֵר מִמֶּנִי?" בְּאוֹתָהּ שָׁעָה נִזְדַּמְּנָה לוֹ צְפַרְדֵּעַ אַחַת וְאָמְרָה לוֹ, דָּוִד! אַל תָּזוּחַ דַּעְתְּךָ עָלֶיךָ, שֶׁאֲנִי אוֹמֶרֶת שִׁירוֹת וְתִשְׁבָּחוֹת יוֹתֵר מִמְּךָ. וְלֹא עוֹד אֶלָּא כָּל שִׁירָה שֶׁאֲנִי אוֹמֶרֶת מְמֻשֶּׁלֶת עָלֶיהָ שְׁלֹשֶׁת אֲלָפִים מָשָׁל שֶׁנֶּאֱמַר (מלכים א ה יב) "וַיְדַבֵּר שְׁלֹשֶׁת אֲלָפִים מָשָׁל וַיְהִי שִׁירוֹ חֲמִשָּׁה וָאָלֶף." וְלֹא עוֹד אֶלָּא שֶׁאֲנִי עוֹסֶקֶת בְּמִצְוָה גְדוֹלָה, וְזוֹ הִיא הַמִּצְוָה שֶׁאֲנִי עוֹסֶקֶת בָּהּ – יֵשׁ בִּשְׂפַת הַיָּם מִין אֶחָד שֶׁאֵין פַּרְנָסָתוֹ כִּי אִם מִן הַמַּיִם וּבְשָׁעָה שֶׁהוּא רָעֵב נוֹטְלַנִי וְאוֹכְלַנִי לְקַיֵּם מַה שֶׁנֶּאֱמַר (משלי כה:כא-כב) "אִם רָעֵב שֹׂנַאֲךָ הַאֲכִילֵהוּ לָחֶם וְאִם צָמֵא הַשְׁקֵהוּ מָיִם כִּי גֶחָלִים אַתָּה חֹתֶה עַל רֹאשׁוֹ וַיהֹוָה יְשַׁלֶּם לָךְ" אַל תִּקְרֵי יְשַׁלֶּם לָךְ אֶלָּא יַשְׁלִימֵהוּ לָךְ:

Chapter One

פרק ראשון

The Heavens are saying: "The heavens speak of G-d's glory, and the skies tell of His handiwork."

שָׁמַיִם אוֹמְרִים. הַשָּׁמַיִם מְסַפְּרִים כְּבוֹד אֵל וּמַעֲשֵׂה יָדָיו מַגִּיד הָרָקִיעַ: (תהלים יט, ב)

The Earth is saying: "The earth and everything in it are G-d's; the inhabited area and all that dwell within it." And it is saying:

אֶרֶץ אוֹמֶרֶת. לְדָוִד מִזְמוֹר לַיהוה הָאָרֶץ וּמְלוֹאָהּ תֵּבֵל וְיֹשְׁבֵי בָהּ:

(תהלים כד א) וְאוֹמֵר. מִכְּנַף הָאָרֶץ זְמִרֹת שָׁמַעְנוּ צְבִי לַצַּדִּיק: (ישעיהו כד טז)	From the wings of the land we have heard song, glory to the righteous."
גַּן עֵדֶן אוֹמֵר. עוּרִי צָפוֹן וּבוֹאִי תֵימָן הָפִיחִי גַנִּי יִזְּלוּ בְשָׂמָיו יָבֹא דוֹדִי לְגַנּוֹ וְיֹאכַל פְּרִי מְגָדָיו: (שיר השירים ד טז)	The Garden of Eden is saying: "Arouse yourself, O' north [wind], and come, O' south! Blow upon my garden, let its spices flow out; let my Beloved come to His garden and eat of its precious fruit."
גֵּיהִנֹּם אוֹמֵר. כִּי הִשְׂבִּיעַ נֶפֶשׁ שֹׁקֵקָה וְנֶפֶשׁ רְעֵבָה מִלֵּא טוֹב: (תהלים קז ט)	Gehinnom is saying: For He has satisfied the longing soul, and has filled the hungry soul with good."
מִדְבָּר אוֹמֵר. יְשֻׂשׂוּם מִדְבָּר וְצִיָּה וְתָגֵל עֲרָבָה וְתִפְרַח כַּחֲבַצָּלֶת: (ישעיהו לה א)	The Wilderness is saying: "The wilderness and the desert shall rejoice, and the arid region shall exult, and blossom like the rose."
שָׂדוֹת אוֹמְרִים. יְהוָה בְּחָכְמָה יָסַד אָרֶץ כּוֹנֵן שָׁמַיִם בִּתְבוּנָה: (משלי ג יט)	The Fields are saying: "G'd founded the land with wisdom; He established the heavens with understanding."
מַיִם אוֹמְרִים. לְקוֹל תִּתּוֹ הֲמוֹן מַיִם בַּשָּׁמַיִם וַיַּעַל נְשִׂאִים מִקְצֵה אָרֶץ בְּרָקִים לַמָּטָר עָשָׂה וַיּוֹצֵא רוּחַ מֵאֹצְרֹתָיו: (ירמיה נא טז)	The Seas are saying: "More than the voices of many waters, than the mighty waves of the sea, G'd on high is mighty."
יַמִּים אוֹמְרִים. מִקֹּלוֹת מַיִם רַבִּים אַדִּירִים מִשְׁבְּרֵי יָם אַדִּיר בַּמָּרוֹם יְהוָה: (תהלים צג ד)	The Waters are saying: "When His voice resounds with a great mass of water in the heavens, and He raises vapors from the ends of the Earth; when He makes lightning amongst the rain, and He brings out the wind from its storehouses."
נְהָרוֹת אוֹמְרִים. נְהָרוֹת יִמְחֲאוּ כָף יַחַד הָרִים יְרַנֵּנוּ: (תהלים צח ח)	The Rivers are saying: "Let the rivers clap their hands, let the mountains sing for joy together!"

מַעְיָנוֹת אוֹמְרִים. וְשָׁרִים כְּחֹלְלִים כָּל מַעְיָנָי: (תהלים פז ז)	The Wellsprings are saying: "And as singers who are like dancers are all those who study You."

פרק שני	**Chapter Two**
יוֹם אוֹמֵר. יוֹם לְיוֹם יַבִּיעַ אֹמֶר וְלַיְלָה לְּלַיְלָה יְחַוֶּה דָּעַת: (תהלים יט ג)	The Day is saying: "Day to day utters speech, and night to night relates knowledge."
לַיְלָה אוֹמֵר. לְהַגִּיד בַּבֹּקֶר חַסְדֶּךָ וֶאֱמוּנָתְךָ בַּלֵּילוֹת: (תהלים צב ג)	The Night is saying: "To speak of His kindness in the morning, and of His faithfulness by nights."
שֶׁמֶשׁ אוֹמֵר. שֶׁמֶשׁ יָרֵחַ עָמַד זְבֻלָה לְאוֹר חִצֶּיךָ יְהַלֵּכוּ לְנֹגַהּ בְּרַק חֲנִיתֶךָ: (חבקוק ג יא)	The Sun is saying: "The sun, [when covered by] the moon, stood in its abode; they speed at the light of Your arrows, and at the shining of Your glittering spear."
יָרֵחַ אוֹמֶרֶת. עָשָׂה יָרֵחַ לְמוֹעֲדִים שֶׁמֶשׁ יָדַע מְבוֹאוֹ: (תהלים קד יט)	The Moon is saying: "He made the moon for the festivals; the sun knows the time of its coming."
כּוֹכָבִים אוֹמְרִים. אַתָּה הוּא יהוה לְבַדֶּךָ אַתָּה עָשִׂיתָ אֶת הַשָּׁמַיִם שְׁמֵי הַשָּׁמַיִם וְכָל צְבָאָם הָאָרֶץ וְכָל אֲשֶׁר עָלֶיהָ הַיַּמִּים וְכָל אֲשֶׁר בָּהֶם וְאַתָּה מְחַיֶּה אֶת כֻּלָּם וּצְבָא הַשָּׁמַיִם לְךָ מִשְׁתַּחֲוִים: (נחמיה ט ו)	The Stars are saying, "You, only You, are G'd; You made heaven, the heaven of heavens, with all their host; the earth, and everything that is in it; the seas, and everything that is in them; and You preserve them all; and the host of heaven prostrate themselves to You."
עָבִים אוֹמְרִים. יָשֶׁת חֹשֶׁךְ סִתְרוֹ סְבִיבוֹתָיו סֻכָּתוֹ חֶשְׁכַת מַיִם עָבֵי שְׁחָקִים: (תהלים יח ב)	The Thick Clouds are saying, "He made darkness His secret place; His pavilion around Him was dark with waters and thick clouds of the skies."
עַנְנֵי כָבוֹד אוֹמְרִים. אַף בְּרִי יַטְרִיחַ עָב יָפִיץ עֲנַן אוֹרוֹ: (איוב לז יא)	The Light Clouds are saying, "Also He burdens the thick cloud with an overflow; the cloud scatters its light."

רוּחַ אוֹמֵר. אָמַר לַצָּפוֹן תֵּנִי וּלְתֵימָן אַל תִּכְלָאִי הָבִיאִי בָנַי מֵרָחוֹק וּבְנוֹתַי מִקְצֵה הָאָרֶץ: (ישעיה מג ו)	The Wind is saying, "I will say to the north, Give up; and to the south, Do not withhold; bring My sons from far, and My daughters from the ends of the earth."
בְּרָקִים אוֹמְרִים. בְּרָקִים לַמָּטָר עָשָׂה מוֹצֵא רוּחַ מֵאוֹצְרוֹ: (תהלים קלה ז)	The Lightning Bolts are saying, "He causes the vapors to ascend from the ends of the earth; He makes lightning for the rain; He brings forth the wind from His storehouses."
טַל אוֹמֵר. אֶהְיֶה כַטַּל לְיִשְׂרָאֵל יִפְרַח כַּשּׁוֹשַׁנָּה וְיַךְ שָׁרָשָׁיו כַּלְּבָנוֹן: (הושע יד ו)	The Dew is saying: "I shall be as the dew to Israel, he shall blossom as a rose, he shall spread forth his roots as the Lebanon." Other texts add: "Arouse yourself O' north [wind], and come, O' south! Blow upon my garden, let its spices flow out; let my Beloved come to His garden and eat of its precious fruit."
גְּשָׁמִים אוֹמְרִים. גֶּשֶׁם נְדָבוֹת תָּנִיף אֱלֹהִים נַחֲלָתְךָ וְנִלְאָה אַתָּה כוֹנַנְתָּ: (תהלים סח י)	The Rains are saying, "You, O' L-rd, poured a generous rain, to strengthen Your heritage when it languished."

פרק שלישי	**Chapter Three**
אִילָנוֹת שֶׁבְּשָׂדֶה אוֹמְרִים. אָז יְרַנְּנוּ עֲצֵי הַיָּעַר מִלְּפְנֵי יהוה כִּי בָא לִשְׁפּוֹט אֶת הָאָרֶץ: (דברי הימים א טז לג)	The Wild Trees are saying, "Then shall the trees of the forest sing out at the presence of G-d, because He comes to judge the earth."
גֶּפֶן אוֹמֶרֶת. כֹּה אָמַר יהוה כַּאֲשֶׁר יִמָּצֵא הַתִּירוֹשׁ בָּאֶשְׁכּוֹל וְאָמַר אַל תַּשְׁחִיתֵהוּ כִּי בְרָכָה בּוֹ כֵּן אֶעֱשֶׂה לְמַעַן עֲבָדַי לְבִלְתִּי הַשְׁחִית הַכֹּל: (ישעיה סה ח)	The Vine is saying, "So says G-d: As the wine is found in the cluster, and one says: Do not destroy it, for a blessing is in it - so shall I do for the sake of my servants, so as not to destroy everything."
תְּאֵנָה אוֹמֶרֶת. נֹצֵר תְּאֵנָה יֹאכַל פִּרְיָהּ: (משלי כז יח)	The Fig is saying: "The one who guards the fig shall eat of her fruits."

רִמוֹן אוֹמֵר. כְּפֶלַח הָרִמוֹן רַקָתֵךְ מִבַּעַד לְצַמָּתֵךְ: (שיר השירים ד ג)	The Pomegranate is saying, "Your cheeks are like a piece of a pomegranate behind your veil."
תָּמָר אוֹמֵר. צַדִּיק כַּתָּמָר יִפְרָח כְּאֶרֶז בַּלְּבָנוֹן יִשְׂגֶּה: (תהלים צב יג)	The Palm is saying, "The righteous flourish like the palm tree; they grow like a cedar in Lebanon."
תַּפּוּחַ אוֹמֵר. כְּתַפּוּחַ בַּעֲצֵי הַיַּעַר כֵּן דּוֹדִי בֵּין הַבָּנִים בְּצִלּוֹ חִמַּדְתִּי וְיָשַׁבְתִּי וּפִרְיוֹ מָתוֹק לְחִכִּי: (שיר השירים ב ג)	The Esrog is saying, "Like the esrog tree among the trees of the wood, so is my beloved among young men. I sat down under his shadow with delight, and his fruit was sweet to my taste."
שִׁבֹּלֶת חִטִּים שִׁיר הַמַּעֲלוֹת מִמַּעֲמַקִּים קְרָאתִיךָ יְהֹוָה: (תהלים קד א)	The Sheaves of Wheat are saying, "A song of ascents: Out of the depths have I cried to You, O' G-d."
שִׁבֹּלֶת שְׂעוֹרִים תְּפִלָּה לְעָנִי כִי יַעֲטֹף וְלִפְנֵי יהוה יִשְׁפֹּךְ שִׂיחוֹ: (תהלים קב א)	The Sheaves of Barley are saying, "A prayer of the pauper, when he swoons, and pours out his speech before G-d."
שְׁאָר הַשִּׁבֳּלִים אוֹמְרִים. לָבְשׁוּ כָרִים הַצֹּאן וַעֲמָקִים יַעַטְפוּ בָר יִתְרוֹעֲעוּ אַף יָשִׁירוּ: (תהלים סה יד)	The Other Sheaves are saying, "The meadows are clothed with flocks; the valleys also are covered over with grain; they shout for joy, they also sing."
יְרָקוֹת שֶׁבַּשָּׂדֶה אוֹמְרִים. תְּלָמֶיהָ רַוֵּה נַחֵת גְּדוּדֶהָ בִּרְבִיבִים תְּמֹגְגֶנָּה צִמְחָהּ תְּבָרֵךְ: (תהלים סה יא)	The Vegetables of the Field are saying, "You water its furrows abundantly; You settle its ridges; you make it soft with showers; You bless its growth."
דְּשָׁאִים אוֹמְרִים. יְהִי כְבוֹד יְהֹוָה לְעוֹלָם יִשְׂמַח יהוה בְּמַעֲשָׂיו: (תהלים קד לא)	The Grasses are saying, "May the glory of G-d endure forever; may G-d rejoice in His works."

פרק רביעי	**Chapter Four**

תַּרְנְגוֹל אוֹמֵר. בְּשָׁעָה שֶׁבָּא הַקָּדוֹשׁ בָּרוּךְ הוּא אֵצֶל הַצַּדִּיקִים בְּגַן עֵדֶן, זוֹלְפִים כֹּל אִילָנֵי גַן עֵדֶן בְּשָׂמִים, וּמְרַנְּנִים וּמְשַׁבְּחִים, וְאָז גַּם הוּא מִתְעוֹרֵר וּמְשַׁבֵּחַ: (זוהר ב קצה:ב, ויקהל	The Rooster is saying, "When the Holy One, blessed be He, comes to the righteous in the Garden of Eden, all the trees in the Garden of Eden scatter their spices, and they rejoice and praise, and then He, too, is aroused and praises."
בְּקוֹל רִאשׁוֹן אוֹמֵר. זֶה דוֹר דֹּרְשָׁו מְבַקְשֵׁי פָנֶיךָ יַעֲקֹב סֶלָה: שְׂאוּ שְׁעָרִים רָאשֵׁיכֶם וְהִנָּשְׂאוּ פִּתְחֵי עוֹלָם וְיָבוֹא מֶלֶךְ הַכָּבוֹד: מִי זֶה מֶלֶךְ הַכָּבוֹד יהוה עִזּוּז וְגִבּוֹר יהוה גִּבּוֹר מִלְחָמָה: (תהלים כד ז-ח)	In its first call it says, "Lift up your heads, O' gates! And be lifted up, O' everlasting doors! And the King of glory shall come in. Who is this King of glory? G-d strong and mighty, G-d mighty in battle!"
בְּקוֹל שֵׁנִי אוֹמֵר. שְׂאוּ שְׁעָרִים רָאשֵׁיכֶם וּשְׂאוּ פִּתְחֵי עוֹלָם וְיָבֹא מֶלֶךְ הַכָּבוֹד: מִי הוּא זֶה מֶלֶךְ הַכָּבוֹד יהוה צְבָאוֹת הוּא מֶלֶךְ הַכָּבוֹד סֶלָה: (תהלים כד ט-י)	In its second call, it says, "Lift up your heads, O' gates! Lift them up, O' everlasting doors! And the King of glory shall come in. Who is He, this King of glory? G-d of hosts, He is the King of glory, Selah!"
בְּקוֹל שְׁלִישִׁי אוֹמֵר. עִמְדוּ צַדִּיקִים וְעִסְקוּ בַּתּוֹרָה, כְּדֵי שֶׁיִּהְיֶה שְׂכַרְכֶם כָּפוּל לָעוֹלָם הַבָּא:	In its third call it says, "Stand, O' righteous ones, and busy yourselves with Torah, so that your reward shall be double in the World-to-Come."
בְּקוֹל רְבִיעִי אוֹמֵר. לִישׁוּעָתְךָ קִוִּיתִי יהוה: (בראשית מט יח)	In its fourth call it says, "I have hoped for your salvation, O' G-d."
בְּקוֹל חֲמִישִׁי אוֹמֵר. עַד מָתַי עָצֵל תִּשְׁכָּב מָתַי תָּקוּם מִשְּׁנָתֶךָ: (משלי ו ט)	In its fifth call, it is saying, "How long will you sleep, O' sluggard? When will you arise from your sleep?"
בְּקוֹל שִׁשִּׁי אוֹמֵר. אַל תֶּאֱהַב שֵׁנָה פֶּן תִּוָּרֵשׁ פְּקַח עֵינֶיךָ שְׂבַע לָחֶם: (משלי כ יג)	In its sixth call, it is saying, "Do not love sleep, lest you come to poverty; open your eyes, and you shall be satisfied with bread."

בְּקוֹל שְׁבִיעִי אוֹמֵר. עֵת לַעֲשׂוֹת לַיהוה הֵפֵרוּ תּוֹרָתֶךָ: (תהלים קיט קכו)	In its seventh call, it is saying, "It is time to act for G-d; for they have made void Your Torah."
תַּרְנְגֹלֶת אוֹמֶרֶת. נֹתֵן לֶחֶם לְכָל בָּשָׂר כִּי לְעוֹלָם חַסְדּוֹ: (תהלים קלו כה)	The Hen is saying, "He gives bread to all flesh, for His kindness endures forever."
יוֹנָה אוֹמֶרֶת. כְּסוּס עָגוּר כֵּן אֲצַפְצֵף אֶהְגֶּה כַּיּוֹנָה דַּלּוּ עֵינַי לַמָּרוֹם אֲדֹנָי עָשְׁקָה לִי עָרְבֵנִי: (ישעיה לח יד) אוֹמֶרֶת יוֹנָה לִפְנֵי הַקָּדוֹשׁ בָּרוּךְ הוּא, רִבּוֹנוֹ שֶׁל עוֹלָם, יִהְיוּ מְזוֹנוֹתַי מְרוֹרִים כְּזַיִת בְּיָדְךָ, וְאַל יִהְיוּ מְתוּקִים כִּדְבַשׁ, עַל יְדֵי בָּשָׂר וָדָם: (ערובין יח ב מד-מה)	The Dove is saying, "Like a swift or crane, so do I chatter; I moan like a dove; my eyes fail with looking upward; O' G-d, I am oppressed, be my senility." The dove says before The Holy One, Blessed be He: "Master of the World! May my sustenance be as bitter as an olive in Your Hand, rather than it being sweet as honey through flesh and blood."
נֶשֶׁר אוֹמֵר. וְאַתָּה יהוה אֱלֹהִים צְבָאוֹת אֱלֹהֵי יִשְׂרָאֵל הָקִיצָה לִפְקֹד כָּל הַגּוֹיִם אַל תָּחֹן כָּל בֹּגְדֵי אָוֶן סֶלָה: (תהלים נט ו)	The Vulture is saying, "And You, G-d, L-RD of Hosts, L-RD of Israel, awake to punish all the nations; do not be gracious to any wicked traitors, sela!"
עָגוּר אוֹמֵר. הוֹדוּ לַיהוה בְּכִנּוֹר בְּנֵבֶל עָשׂוֹר זַמְּרוּ לוֹ: (תהלים לג ב)	The Crane is saying, "Give thanks to G-d with the lyre, make music for Him with the ten-stringed harp."
צִפּוֹר אוֹמֵר. גַּם צִפּוֹר מָצְאָה בַיִת וּדְרוֹר קֵן לָהּ אֲשֶׁר שָׁתָה אֶפְרֹחֶיהָ אֶת מִזְבְּחוֹתֶיךָ יהוה צְבָאוֹת מַלְכִּי וֵאלֹהָי: (תהלים פד ד)	The Songbird is saying, "The songbird has also found her home, and the sparrow a nest for herself, where she may lay her young - Your altars, G-d of Hosts, my King and my L-rd."
סְנוּנִית אוֹמֶרֶת. לְמַעַן יְזַמֶּרְךָ כָבוֹד וְלֹא יִדֹּם יהוה אֱלֹהַי לְעוֹלָם אוֹדֶךָ: (תהלים לג יג)	The Swallow is saying, "So that my soul shall praise You, and shall not be silent, G-d my L-RD, I shall give thanks to You forever."
טַסִית אוֹמֶרֶת. עֶזְרִי מֵעִם יהוה עֹשֵׂה שָׁמַיִם וָאָרֶץ: (תהלים קכא ב)	The Swift is saying: "My help is from G-d, Maker of Heaven and earth."

צִיָּה אוֹמֶרֶת. אוֹר זָרֻעַ לַצַּדִּיק וּלְיִשְׁרֵי לֵב שִׂמְחָה: (תהלים צז יב)	The Stormy Petrel is saying: "Light is sown for the righteous, and joy for the straight-hearted."
רְצָפִי אוֹמֵר. נַחֲמוּ נַחֲמוּ עַמִּי יֹאמַר אֱלֹהֵיכֶם: (ישעיה מ א)	The Laughing Dove is saying: "Comfort My people, comfort them, says your L-rd."
חֲסִידָה אוֹמֶרֶת. דַּבְּרוּ עַל לֵב יְרוּשָׁלַָם וְקִרְאוּ אֵלֶיהָ כִּי מָלְאָה צְבָאָהּ כִּי נִרְצָה עֲוֹנָהּ כִּי לָקְחָה מִיַּד יהוה כִּפְלַיִם בְּכָל חַטֹּאתֶיהָ: (ישעיה מ ב)	The Stork is saying: "Speak to the heart of Jerusalem, and call to her, for her time has arrived, for her sins have been pardoned, for she has taken double from G-d's hand for all her sins."
עוֹרֵב אוֹמֵר. מִי יָכִין לָעֹרֵב צֵידוֹ כִּי יְלָדָיו אֶל אֵל יְשַׁוֵּעוּ: (איוב לח מא)	The Raven is saying, "Who prepares food for the raven, when his young ones cry out to G-d?"
זַרְזִיר אוֹמֵר. נוֹדַע בַּגּוֹיִם זַרְעָם וְצֶאֱצָאֵיהֶם בְּתוֹךְ הָעַמִּים כָּל רֹאֵיהֶם יַכִּירוּם כִּי הֵם זֶרַע בֵּרַךְ יהוה: (ישעיה סא ט)	The Starling is saying, "Their seed shall be known among the nations, and their offspring among the peoples; all who see them shall acknowledge them, that they are the seed which G-d has blessed."
אֲוָז שֶׁבַּבַּיִת אוֹמֶרֶת. הוֹדוּ לַיהוה קִרְאוּ בִשְׁמוֹ הוֹדִיעוּ בָעַמִּים עֲלִילוֹתָיו: שִׁירוּ לוֹ זַמְּרוּ לוֹ שִׂיחוּ בְּכָל נִפְלְאוֹתָיו: (תהלים קה א-ב)	The Domestic Goose is saying, "Give thanks to G-d, call upon His Name, make His works known amongst the peoples, sing to Him, make music for Him, speak of all His wonders."
אֲוָז הַבָּר הַמְשׁוֹטֶטֶת בַּמִּדְבָּר כְּשֶׁרוֹאָה אֶת יִשְׂרָאֵל עוֹסְקִים בַּתּוֹרָה אוֹמֶרֶת. קוֹל קוֹרֵא בַּמִּדְבָּר, פַּנּוּ דֶּרֶךְ יהוה, יַשְּׁרוּ בָּעֲרָבָה מְסִלָּה לֵאלֹהֵינוּ: (ישעיה מ ג) וְעַל מְצִיאוּת מְזוֹנוֹתֶיהָ בַּמִּדְבָּר אוֹמֶרֶת. אָרוּר הַגֶּבֶר אֲשֶׁר יִבְטַח בָּאָדָם, בָּרוּךְ הַגֶּבֶר אֲשֶׁר יִבְטַח בַּיהוה וְהָיָה יהוה מִבְטַחוֹ: (ירמיה יז:ה-ז)	The Wild Goose flying in the wilderness, when it sees Israel busy with Torah, is saying, "A voice cries, Prepare in the wilderness the way of G-d, make straight in the desert a path for our G-d." And upon finding its food in the wilderness, it says, "Cursed is the man who trusts in human beings… Blessed is the man who trusts in G-d, and G-d shall be his assurance."

פְּרוֹגִיּוֹת אוֹמְרִים. בִּטְחוּ בַיהוה עֲדֵי עַד כִּי בְּיָהּ יהוה צוּר עוֹלָמִים: (ישעיה כו ד)	The Ducks are saying, "Trust in G-d forever and ever, for G-d, the Eternal, is the strength of worlds."
רַחֲמָה אוֹמֶרֶת. אֶשְׁרְקָה לָהֶם וַאֲקַבְּצֵם כִּי פְדִיתִים וְרָבוּ כְּמוֹ רָבוּ: (זכריה י ח)	The Bee-Eater is saying: "I will whistle to them and gather them, for I have redeemed them, and they shall increase as they have before increased."
צִפֹּרֶת כְּרָמִים אוֹמֶרֶת. אֶשָּׂא עֵינַי אֶל הֶהָרִים מֵאַיִן יָבֹא עֶזְרִי: (תהלים קכא א)	The Grasshopper is saying: "I lift my eyes up to the mountains, where shall my help come from?"
חָסִיל אוֹמֵר. יהוה אֱלֹהַי אַתָּה אֲרוֹמִמְךָ אוֹדֶה שִׁמְךָ כִּי עָשִׂיתָ פֶּלֶא עֵצוֹת מֵרָחוֹק אֱמוּנָה אֹמֶן: (ישעיה כה א)	The Locust is saying, "O' G-d, You are my L-rd; I will exalt You, I will praise Your Name; for You have done wondrous things; Your counsels of old are faithfulness and truth."
שְׁמָמִית אוֹמֶרֶת. הַלְלוּהוּ בְצִלְצְלֵי שָׁמַע הַלְלוּהוּ בְּצִלְצְלֵי תְרוּעָה: (תהלים קנ ה)	The Spider is saying, "Praise Him with sounding cymbals! Praise Him with loud clashing cymbals!"
זְבוּב אוֹמֵר. בְּשָׁעָה שֶׁאֵין יִשְׂרָאֵל עוֹסְקִים בַּתּוֹרָה, קוֹל אֹמֵר קְרָא וְאָמַר מָה אֶקְרָא כָּל הַבָּשָׂר חָצִיר וְכָל חַסְדּוֹ כְּצִיץ הַשָּׂדֶה: יָבֵשׁ חָצִיר נָבֵל צִיץ כִּי רוּחַ יהוה נָשְׁבָה בּוֹ אָכֵן חָצִיר הָעָם: יָבֵשׁ חָצִיר נָבֵל צִיץ וּדְבַר אֱלֹהֵינוּ יָקוּם לְעוֹלָם: (ישעיה מ ו-ח) בּוֹרֵא נִיב שְׂפָתָיִם שָׁלוֹם שָׁלוֹם לָרָחוֹק וְלַקָּרוֹב אָמַר יהוה וּרְפָאתִיו: (ישעיה נז יט)	The Fly, when Israel is not busying itself with Torah, is saying, "The voice said, 'Call out.' And he said, 'What shall I call out? All flesh is grass, and all its grace is as the flower of the field.' '…The grass withers, the flower fades; but the word of our L-RD shall endure forever. "I will create a new expression of the lips; Peace, peace for him who is far off and for him who is near, says G-d; and I will heal him."
תַּנִּינִים אוֹמְרִים. הַלְלוּ אֶת יהוה מִן הָאָרֶץ תַּנִּינִים וְכָל תְּהֹמוֹת: (תהלים קמח ז)	The Sea Monsters are saying: "Praise G-d from the land, the sea monsters and all the depths."

לִוְיָתָן אוֹמֵר. הוֹדוּ לַיהוה כִּי טוֹב כִּי לְעוֹלָם חַסְדּוֹ: (תהלים קלו א)	The Leviathan is saying, "Give thanks to G-d for He is good, for His kindness endures forever."
דָּגִים אוֹמְרִים. קוֹל יהוה עַל הַמָּיִם אֵל הַכָּבוֹד הִרְעִים יהוה עַל מַיִם רַבִּים: (תהלים כט ג)	The Fishes are saying, "The voice of G-d is upon the waters, the G-d of glory thunders, G-d is upon many waters."
צְפַרְדֵּעַ אוֹמֶרֶת. בָּרוּךְ שֵׁם כְּבוֹד מַלְכוּתוֹ לְעוֹלָם וָעֶד: (פסחים נו א)	The Frog is saying, Blessed is the Name of the honor of His Kingdom for all eternity."

פרק חמישי	**Chapter Five**
בְּהֵמָה דַּקָּה טְהוֹרָה אוֹמֶרֶת. מִי כָמֹכָה בָּאֵלִם יהוה מִי כָּמֹכָה נֶאְדָּר בַּקֹּדֶשׁ נוֹרָא תְהִלֹּת עֹשֵׂה פֶלֶא: (שמות טו יא)	The Sheep is saying: "Who is like You among the mighty ones, G-d, who is like You, mighty in holiness, awesome in praise, worker of wonders."
בְּהֵמָה גַּסָּה טְהוֹרָה אוֹמֶרֶת. הַרְנִינוּ לֵאלֹהִים עוּזֵּנוּ הָרִיעוּ לֵאלֹהֵי יַעֲקֹב: (תהלים פא ב)	The Cow is saying: "Rejoice to the L-rd over our strength, trumpet to the L-rd of Yaakov!"
בְּהֵמָה דַּקָּה טְמֵאָה אוֹמֶרֶת. הֵיטִיבָה יהוה לַטּוֹבִים וְלִישָׁרִים בְּלִבּוֹתָם: (תהלים קכה ד)	The Pig is saying: "G-d is good to the good, and to the straight-hearted."
בְּהֵמָה גַּסָּה טְמֵאָה אוֹמֶרֶת. יְגִיעַ כַּפֶּיךָ כִּי תֹאכֵל אַשְׁרֶיךָ וְטוֹב לָךְ: (תהלים קכח ב)	The Beast of Burden is saying: "When you eat the fruit of your labors, happy are you and good is your lot."
גָּמָל אוֹמֵר. יהוה מִמָּרוֹם יִשְׁאָג וּמִמְּעוֹן קָדְשׁוֹ יִתֵּן קוֹלוֹ שָׁאֹג יִשְׁאַג עַל נָוֵהוּ: (ירמיה כה ל)	The Camel is saying: "G-d shall roar from upon high and cause His voice to sound forth from His holy place, His shout echoes profoundly over His dwelling place."
סוּס אוֹמֵר. הִנֵּה כְעֵינֵי עֲבָדִים אֶל יַד אֲדוֹנֵיהֶם כְּעֵינֵי שִׁפְחָה אֶל יַד	The Horse is saying: "Behold, as the eyes of the servants to the hand of their master, as the eyes of the maidservant to the hand of her

גְּבִרְתָּהּ כֵּן עֵינֵינוּ אֶל יהוה אֱלֹהֵינוּ עַד שֶׁיְּחָנֵנוּ: (תהלים קכג ב)	mistress, so are our eyes to G-d our L-rd until He will favor us."
פֶּרֶד אוֹמֵר. יוֹדוּךָ יהוה כָּל מַלְכֵי אֶרֶץ כִּי שָׁמְעוּ אִמְרֵי פִיךָ: (תהלים קלח ד)	The Mule is saying, "All the kings of the earth shall acknowledge You, G-d, for they have heard the sayings of Your mouth."
חֲמוֹר אוֹמֵר. לְךָ יהוה הַגְּדֻלָּה וְהַגְּבוּרָה וְהַתִּפְאֶרֶת וְהַנֵּצַח וְהַהוֹד כִּי כֹל בַּשָּׁמַיִם וּבָאָרֶץ לְךָ יהוה הַמַּמְלָכָה וְהַמִּתְנַשֵּׂא לְכֹל לְרֹאשׁ: (דברי הימים א, כט יא)	The Donkey is saying: "Yours, G-d, is the greatness, and the might, and the splendor, and the victory, and the glory, for everything in the Heavens and earth [is Yours]; Yours, G-d, is the kingship, and the exaltation over all."
שׁוֹר אוֹמֵר. אָז יָשִׁיר מֹשֶׁה וּבְנֵי יִשְׂרָאֵל אֶת הַשִּׁירָה הַזֹּאת לַיהוה וַיֹּאמְרוּ לֵאמֹר אָשִׁירָה לַיהוה כִּי גָאֹה גָּאָה סוּס וְרֹכְבוֹ רָמָה בַיָּם: (שמות טו א)	The Ox is saying, "Then Moshe and the Children of Israel sang this song to G-d, and they said, I shall sing to G-d, for He has triumphed; He has thrown the horse and its rider into the sea."
חַיּוֹת הַשָּׂדֶה אוֹמְרִים. בָּרוּךְ הַטּוֹב וְהַמֵּטִיב: (ברכות מח ב)	The Wild Animals are saying, "Blessed is the One Who is good and bestows good."
צְבִי אוֹמֵר. וַאֲנִי אָשִׁיר עֻזֶּךָ וַאֲרַנֵּן לַבֹּקֶר חַסְדֶּךָ כִּי הָיִיתָ מִשְׂגָּב לִי וּמָנוֹס בְּיוֹם צַר לִי: (תהלים נט יז)	The Gazelle is saying: "And I shall sing of Your strength, I shall rejoice of Your kindness in the morning, for You were a refuge to me, and a hiding place on the day of my oppression."
פִּיל אוֹמֵר. מַה גָּדְלוּ מַעֲשֶׂיךָ יהוה מְאֹד עָמְקוּ מַחְשְׁבֹתֶיךָ: (תהלים צב ו)	The Elephant is saying: "How great are Your works, G-d; Your thoughts are tremendously deep."
אַרְיֵה אוֹמֵר יהוה כַּגִּבּוֹר יֵצֵא כְּאִישׁ מִלְחָמוֹת יָעִיר קִנְאָה יָרִיעַ אַף יַצְרִיחַ עַל אֹיְבָיו יִתְגַּבָּר: (ישעיה מב יג)	The Lion is saying: "G-d shall go out as a mighty man, He shall arouse zeal He shall say, even roar, He shall prevail over His enemies."
דֹּב אוֹמֵר. יִשְׂאוּ מִדְבָּר וְעָרָיו חֲצֵרִים תֵּשֵׁב קֵדָר יָרֹנּוּ יֹשְׁבֵי סֶלַע	The Bear is saying: "Let the wilderness and its cities lift up their voice, the village that

מֵרֹאשׁ הָרִים יִצְוָחוּ: (ישעיה מב יא)	Kedar inhabits; let the inhabitants of the rocks sing, let them shout from the peaks of the mountains. Let them give glory to G-d, and tell of His praise in the islands."
זְאֵב אוֹמֵר. עַל כָּל דְּבַר פֶּשַׁע עַל שׁוֹר עַל חֲמוֹר עַל שֶׂה עַל שַׂלְמָה עַל כָּל אֲבֵדָה אֲשֶׁר יֹאמַר כִּי הוּא זֶה עַד הָאֱלֹהִים יָבֹא דְּבַר שְׁנֵיהֶם אֲשֶׁר יַרְשִׁיעֻן אֱלֹהִים יְשַׁלֵּם שְׁנַיִם לְרֵעֵהוּ: (שמות כב ח)	The Wolf is saying: "For every matter of iniquity, for the ox, the donkey, the lamb, the garment, for every lost item about which he says, 'This is it,' the matter of both of them shall come before the judge; he who the judge finds guilty shall pay double to the other."
שׁוּעָל אוֹמֵר. הוֹי בֹּנֶה בֵיתוֹ בְּלֹא צֶדֶק וַעֲלִיּוֹתָיו בְּלֹא מִשְׁפָּט בְּרֵעֵהוּ יַעֲבֹד חִנָּם וּפֹעֲלוֹ לֹא יִתֶּן לוֹ: (ירמיה כב יג)	The Fox is saying: "Woe to him that builds his house without justice, and his chambers without lawfulness; that uses his friend's service without wages, and does not give him for his hire."
זַרְזִיר אוֹמֵר. רַנְּנוּ צַדִּיקִים בַּיהוָה לַיְשָׁרִים נָאוָה תְהִלָּה: (תהלים לג א)	The Hound is saying, "Let the righteous rejoice in G-d, praise is befitting to the straight."
חָתוּל אוֹמֵר. אֶרְדּוֹף אוֹיְבַי וְאַשִּׂיגֵם וְלֹא אָשׁוּב עַד כַּלּוֹתָם: (תהלים יח לח)	The Cat is saying, "If you rise up like a vulture, and place your nest among the stars, from there I shall bring you down, says G-d."
עַכְבָּר אוֹמֵר. אֲרוֹמִמְךָ יְהוָה כִּי דִלִּיתָנִי וְלֹא שִׂמַּחְתָּ אֹיְבַי לִי: (תהלים לב)	And The Mouse says, "I shall exalt you, G-d, for You have impoverished me, and You have not let my enemies rejoice over me."
וּכְשֶׁמַּגִּיעוֹ אוֹמֵר הַחָתוּל. אֶרְדּוֹף אוֹיְבַי וְאַשִּׂיגֵם וְלֹא אָשׁוּב עַד כַּלּוֹתָם: (תהלים יח לח)	And when the cat catches it, the cat says, "I have pursued my enemies and overtaken them, and I did not return until they were destroyed."
וְהָעַכְבָּר אוֹמֵר. וְאַתָּה צַדִּיק עַל כָּל הַבָּא עָלַי כִּי אֱמֶת עָשִׂיתָ וַאֲנִי הִרְשָׁעְתִּי: (נחמיה ט לג)	And the mouse says, "You are just for all that comes upon me, for You have acted truthfully, and I have been wicked."

פרק ששי	Chapter Six
שְׁרָצִים אוֹמְרִים. יִשְׂמַח יִשְׂרָאֵל בְּעֹשָׂיו בְּנֵי צִיּוֹן יָגִילוּ בְמַלְכָּם: (תהלים קמט ב)	The Creeping Creatures are saying, "Let Israel rejoice in He Who made him; let the children of Zion be joyful in their King." Alternate version: "May the glory of G-d endure forever; may G-d rejoice in His works."
אֵלִים שֶׁבַּשְּׁרָצִים אוֹמְרִים. אֶשְׁתְּךָ כְּגֶפֶן פֹּרִיָּה בְּיַרְכְּתֵי בֵיתֶךָ בָּנֶיךָ כִּשְׁתִלֵי זֵיתִים סָבִיב לְשֻׁלְחָנֶךָ: (תהלים קכח ג)	The Prolific Creeping Creatures are saying, "Your wife shall be like a fruitful vine in the recesses of your house; your children like olive shoots around your table."
נָחָשׁ אוֹמֵר. סוֹמֵךְ יהוה לְכָל הַנֹּפְלִים וְזוֹקֵף לְכָל הַכְּפוּפִים: (תהלים קמה יד)	The Snake is saying, "G-d supports all the fallen, and straightens all the bent."
עַקְרָב אוֹמֵר. טוֹב יהוה לַכֹּל וְרַחֲמָיו עַל כָּל מַעֲשָׂיו: (תהלים קמה ט)	The Scorpion is saying, "G-d is good to all, and His mercy is upon all of His handiwork."
שַׁבְלוּל אוֹמֵר. כְּמוֹ שַׁבְּלוּל תֶּמֶס יַהֲלֹךְ נֵפֶל אֵשֶׁת בַּל חָזוּ שָׁמֶשׁ: (תהלים נח ט)	The Snail is saying, "Like the snail that melts away, the stillborn of a mole that does not see the sun."
נְמָלָה אוֹמֶרֶת. לֵךְ אֶל נְמָלָה עָצֵל רְאֵה דְרָכֶיהָ וַחֲכָם: (ספר משלי ו ו)	The Ant it is saying, "Go to the ant, you sluggard; consider her ways, and be wise."
חֻלְדָּה אוֹמֶרֶת. כֹּל הַנְּשָׁמָה תְּהַלֵּל יָהּ הַלְלוּיָהּ: (תהלים קנ ו)	The Rat is saying, "Let every soul praise G-d, Halleluyah!"
כְּלָבִים אוֹמְרִים. בֹּאוּ נִשְׁתַּחֲוֶה וְנִכְרָעָה נִבְרְכָה לִפְנֵי יהוה עֹשֵׂנוּ: (תהלים צה ו)	The Dogs are saying, "Come, let us worship and bow down; let us kneel before G-d our Maker."

[Yalkut Shimoni, Bo 187:] Rabbi Yeshayah, a student of Rabbi Ḥanina ben Dosa, fasted eighty-five fasts. He said, Dogs, about which it is written, "The dogs are brazen of spirit; they do not know satisfaction" - shall they merit saying a song? An angel answered him from Heaven and said to him, Yeshayah, until when will you fast over this? It is an oath from the Holy One, Blessed is He; from the day that He revealed His secret to Havakuk the prophet, He has not revealed this matter to anyone in the world. But because you are the student of a great man, I have been sent from Heaven to assist you. They said that dogs have written about them, "No dog sharpened its tongue against any of the children of Israel". Furthermore, they merited that hides are tanned with their excrement, on which Tefillin, Mezuzos, and Torah scrolls are written. For this reason, they merited saying a song. And regarding what you asked, take back your word and do not continue in this way, as it is written, "He that guards his mouth and tongue, guards from afflictions of his soul."

(יַלְקוּט שִׁמְעוֹנִי פָּרָשַׁת בֹּא רֶמֶז קפ"ז) רַבִּי יְשַׁעְיָה תַּלְמִידוֹ שֶׁל רַבִּי חֲנִינָא בֶּן דּוֹסָא הִתְעַנָּה חָמֵשׁ וּשְׁמוֹנִים תַּעֲנִיּוֹת. אָמַר כְּלָבִים שֶׁכָּתוּב בָּהֶם (יְשַׁעְיָה נ"ו י"א) וְהַכְּלָבִים עַזֵּי נֶפֶשׁ לֹא יָדְעוּ שָׂבְעָה, יִזְכּוּ לוֹמַר שִׁירָה. עָנָה לוֹ מַלְאָךְ מִן הַשָּׁמַיִם וְאָמַר לוֹ יְשַׁעְיָה עַד מָתַי אַתָּה מִתְעַנֶּה עַל זֶה הַדָּבָר שֶׁבּוּעָה הִיא מִלִּפְנֵי הַמָּקוֹם בָּרוּךְ הוּא מִיּוֹם שֶׁגִּילָה סוֹדוֹ לַחֲבַקּוּק הַנָּבִיא לֹא גִלָּה דָבָר זֶה לְשׁוּם בְּרִיָּה בָּעוֹלָם. אֶלָּא בִּשְׁבִיל שֶׁתַּלְמִידוֹ שֶׁל אָדָם גָּדוֹל אַתָּה שְׁלָחוּנִי מִן הַשָּׁמַיִם לְזָדְקֵק אֵלֶיךָ לְהַגִּיד לְךָ בַּמֶּה זָכוּ הַכְּלָבִים לוֹמַר שִׁירָה. לְפִי שֶׁכָּתוּב בָּהֶם (שְׁמוֹת י"א ז) וּלְכֹל בְּנֵי יִשְׂרָאֵל לֹא יֶחֱרַץ כֶּלֶב לְשׁוֹנוֹ. וְלֹא עוֹד אֶלָּא שֶׁזָּכוּ לְעַבֵּד עוֹרוֹת מִצּוֹאָתָם שֶׁכּוֹתְבִים בָּהֶם תְּפִילִּין וּמְזוּזוֹת וְסִפְרֵי תּוֹרָה. עַל כֵּן זָכוּ לוֹמַר שִׁירָה. וּלְעִנְיַן הַשְּׁאֵלָה שֶׁשָּׁאַלְתָּ חֲזוֹר לַאֲחֹרֶיךָ וְאַל תּוֹסִיף בַּדָּבָר הַזֶּה עוֹד, כְּמוֹ שֶׁכָּתוּב (מִשְׁלֵי כ"א כ"ג) שׁוֹמֵר פִּיו וּלְשׁוֹנוֹ שׁוֹמֵר מִצָּרוֹת נַפְשׁוֹ.

Blessed is YHVH forever, Amen and Amen. Blessed is YHVH from Tsiyon, Dweller in Jerusalem, praise Yah! Blessed is YHVH Elohim, Eloah of Israel, worker of wonders alone. And blessed is the Name of His *kavod*, and His *kavod* should fill the entire land, Amen and Amen.

בָּרוּךְ יְהוָה לְעוֹלָם אָמֵן וְאָמֵן: בָּרוּךְ יְהוָה מִצִּיּוֹן שֹׁכֵן יְרוּשָׁלִָם הַלְלוּיָהּ: בָּרוּךְ יְהוָה אֱלֹהִים אֱלֹהֵי יִשְׂרָאֵל עֹשֵׂה נִפְלָאוֹת לְבַדּוֹ: וּבָרוּךְ שֵׁם כְּבוֹדוֹ לְעוֹלָם וְיִמָּלֵא כְבוֹדוֹ אֶת כָּל הָאָרֶץ אָמֵן וְאָמֵן:

Reb Moshe Steinerman
Translation by Rabbi Natan Slifkin.

46812201R00085